ONE HOLY PASSION

The consuming thirst to know God

R.C.SPROUL

publishers since 1798

THOMAS NELSON PUBLISHERS

Nashville • Camden • Kansas City

Published in Nashville, Tennessee, by Thomas Nelson, Inc., and distributed in Canada by Lawson Falle, Ltd., Cambridge, Ontario.

Printed in the United States of America.

Scripture quotations are from THE NEW KING JAMES VERSION of the Bible. Copyright © 1979, 1980, 1982, Thomas Nelson, Inc., Publishers.

Library of Congress Cataloging-in-Publication Data

Sproul, R. C. (Robert Charles), 1939-
  One holy passion.

  1. God.   I. Title.
BT102.S64   1987   231   87-1617
ISBN 0-8407-3049-7

5 6 7 8 9 10 - 97 96 95 94 93 92 91 90 89

For my friends,
Luder and Mary Lou Whitlock
and
Cobby and Lisa Ware.

Contents

Foreword   1

Preface   3

1   Who Are You, God?   5

2   Who Made You, God? 15

3   I Want to Find You, God. 27

4   I Can't See You, God. 43

5   How Much Do You Know, God? 61

6   Where Is Truth, God? 71

7   The Shadow Doesn't Turn 85

8   The Just Judge 105

9   The Invincible Power 125

10   Can I Trust You, God? 143

11   The Love That Will Not Let Us Go 159

12   The Name above All Names 173

Foreword

I have said in print before, and having read this book I now say again, that if I were the devil I would make a special point of trying to stop R. C. Sproul (pronounced *Sprole*, by the way; get it right; he cares!). For R. C. is a man who not only believes God's revealed truth but spreads it; and in spreading it, not only does he make it clear, but he makes sense of it; and the sense he makes of it is not just abstract and theoretical coherence but a practical, moral, down-to-earth, life-changing challenge. Charles Simeon held that the pulpit should relay "the good sense of good men." Well, here in R. C.'s preaching on paper is good sense that could and should revolutionize us all. R. C. is a cross between Puck and Merlin (Frodo and Gandalf, if you prefer), and the lively freshness with which he states things is wonderfully enriching. If the devil does not see that men like R. C. are from his standpoint dangerous, he is a bigger fool than we thought.

This is R. C.'s second volume on God's attributes, meaning His being and character. Having scraped the surface of this theme myself, I venture to say that no topic is greater, grander, or more important, and by the same token none is more demanding. It is a theological Mount Everest, and no one ever masters it or does it full justice. But all that is written here seems to me right-minded and momentous, and I am very grateful for it.

R. C. is a full-blooded believer, with no halfway houses in his thought. He does not dilute the supernaturalism either of

1

the Bible or of the God whose portrait it draws. He is no God-shrinker, as so many are these days, nor does he try to tame God. R. C. does not forget that though in character terms God is Jesuslike, in His own being He is like nothing on earth; so he declines to scale God down to our measure. In this he is correct. Ideas of God fashioned in man's image are idolatrous fancies, not spiritual facts. Would you learn to honor and praise and trust and love the real God, the God who dwells in impenetrable darkness and unapproachable light, the God and Father of our Lord Jesus Christ who becomes our God and Father in and through Him? Read on, then; R. C. is just the guide you need.

J. I. Packer

Preface

One holy passion.

A passion is a strong feeling, an emotion that is packed with intensity. At times it carries a sense of urgency.

Not all passions are holy. As fallen human beings we are often trapped in unholy passions. Our feelings are mixed. Then the Holy Spirit quickens us to a new life with new passions. But many of the old passions remain. We struggle with our feelings. Our affection for the things of God is locked in mortal combat with earthly concerns.

If we are to progress in godliness we need to fan the flames of a holy passion. We need a single-minded desire to know God. We follow Jesus who went before us. He was moved by a single passion—to do the will of His Father. His meat and drink were to do His Father's will. Zeal for His Father's house consumed Him. He was a man of holy destiny with a face set as a flint.

Jesus knew the Father. His knowledge of God was so deep, so profound that His entire earthly life reflected a single holy passion. Jesus revealed the Father to us and called us to imitate His own pursuit. His priority is set before us—to seek first the Kingdom of God and His righteousness.

We are to press into the Kingdom of God, to storm it if we must, to seize the opportunity to know God. This quest is not casual. The pursuit is not cavalier. We are to be driven by a holy passion.

This book is not written for scholars. I have endeavored to write simply yet clearly about complex matters. I have tried to amplify abstract concepts with concrete illustrations and anecdotes drawn from daily life.

A brief word is in order to explain why this book was written. For several years I have had the privilege of teaching theology, the doctrine of God, to seminary students at Reformed Theological Seminary in Jackson, Mississippi. The course has been a source of both delight and frustration for me. My delight has been in seeing many students undergo a profound spiritual experience from a serious study of the doctrine of God. My frustration has been the thought—*Why should such study be reserved for professional clergy? Why do we keep our church laypeople from serious studies of the character of God?*

I realize that a formal course in theology at a seminary offers teaching opportunities that cannot be equaled in a book like this. In the seminary weeks of lectures can be given to a captive audience. The students are required to read weighty books on the subject and submit to regular examinations.

We all know that adult education in the church is not as rigorous as a formal seminary. But is that a valid reason to shrink from a serious study of the character of God?

The goal of this book is not to communicate the kind of knowledge that puffs up, but the kind of knowledge that edifies the soul. I hope God will use it to spark a holy passion in the reader to learn more about God.

Special thanks are in order for the people at Thomas Nelson Publishers who encouraged me to undertake this task. I am particularly indebted to Bruce Nygren for his help. My wife, Vesta, gets credit for making me cut several abstract sections from the book that she judged to be entirely too philosophical. Her lethal red pen makes my writing far less weighty and far more readable. Finally, I express my earnest gratitude to my secretary, Mrs. Maureen Buchman, for her assistance in preparing the manuscript.

Who Are You, God?

I remember Saturday mornings. No school bells, no boring classes, no peanut butter and jelly sandwiches for lunch. No having to sit still without fidgeting. On Saturday I could release the week's worth of energy trapped inside my eight-year-old body.

On Saturdays I played with my dad. Other children were fine playmates the rest of the week, but Saturday was special. This was the day Dad was home.

Our ritual began early. I awakened at the crack of dawn, tiptoed downstairs, and slipped quietly into my parents' bedroom. Father was still asleep. I gently poked my index finger into his ribs. The jab carried a message: "I'm here, Dad."

On cue he lifted the covers and, without opening his eyes, reached out a mammoth arm and scooped me up onto the bed beside him. Dad squeezed me to his side, nearly crushing me with his strength. His night's growth of beard felt like a rough-hewn board against my smooth skin.

I loved it. In his hug I felt his love. His beard scratched and the squeezing hug left me breathless, but I didn't mind; I was safe. As long as he held me tightly, nothing in all the world could hurt me. He loved me and was watching over me. He was there—every Saturday morning.

One night I panicked. I was flirting with sleep when suddenly a chilling thought burst into my mind, *What if my parents die?* A pain began to ache in my stomach. I was old enough to recognize the feeling—*fear*.

I threw off the covers and hurried downstairs, and knocked with a staccato burst on my parents' bedroom door. When Mother opened the door, she looked at me with a puzzled expression. In tears I sobbed out, "Please don't die!"

They understood my fear. Mother held me until my sobbing stopped. Both of them comforted me and assured me that they would not die for a long, long time.

They were wrong. It was not a long, long time. Within seven years the happy magical ritual of Saturday mornings ceased and was replaced by a grim daily ritual. Each evening at dinner time I went to my father's room. There, in an overstuffed chair, he sat, only a shadow of his former self. Gray stubble covered his chin, and his hair was snow white. His hands shook with tremors and one eye was canted aside, out of focus. His lower lip hung at a grotesque angle. Three cerebral strokes had decimated his vibrant strength. He was just fifty-one years old.

Trembling, Dad stretched out his arms toward me. I grasped his wrists and pulled him to his feet. He stood, uncertain, precariously, as I turned my back to him and locked his arms around my neck. I leaned forward, taking his weight on my back, and dragged him to the table for dinner.

Soon the daily ritual ended once and for all. A fourth stroke mercifully claimed Dad's life. I found myself standing at the graveside, the edge of the dark hole camouflaged by a cheap runner of imitation grass. In the distance cemetery workers, dressed in coveralls, leaned indifferently on their shovels. Like vultures they hovered in the background, waiting for the perfunctory ceremony to end so they could close the grave and get on with their daily work.

I watched the minister standing at the head of the grave. As he uttered a litany of the dead, his voice rose above the sounds of the wind and nearby traffic. In his left hand he held a small, black book with gold embossed lettering that read *Book of Common Worship*. His right hand was closed, its contents concealed.

I heard few of his words; my attention was fixed on his right hand. Finally, nearing the end of his litany, the minister dramatically stretched forth his right hand and slowly opened his fist. Sand began to trickle from his fingers and fell on the lid of the coffin, forming a cross. "Earth to earth . . . dust to dust . . . ashes to ashes . . ." were his final words.

Final. The word played on my brain like a record stuck in a groove. Final. *Final*. FINAL.

The minister gently guided my mother away from the grave to a waiting car. I moved behind them in a grim stupor. I was confused. I was hurt. I was angry. One question pierced my soul, a question destined to become an obsession for me; it would soon emerge in my life as a single holy passion. Like Ahab in mad pursuit of an albino whale, I was stricken with a maniacal desire to find out: *Who are you, God? And why do you do the things you do?*

The Ultimate Search

A man lived thousands of years ago who was puzzled by the same kind of questions that bothered me. He was born shortly after a brutal king ordered that all male children be put to death. His mother hid the child for three months but when she could no longer protect him, in desperation she placed him in a small boat and hid him along the bank of a river. The baby was discovered by none other than the cruel king's daughter. She had compassion on the infant and took him home to the royal palace. There she reared the child as her own, carefully concealing his identity from her bloodthirsty father.

The lad grew strong. He was educated by the most advanced tutors of the world and was trained in the ways of royalty. His lifestyle was plush. He lived as a privileged prince, and his destiny for greatness seemed secure.

A rash act changed everything. One day the young prince saw one of the royal guards beating a peasant slave. The prince, boiling with rage at the sight of this obvious injustice, struck the guard violently. The rage turned to fear when the guard slumped at his feet like a rag doll—dead. Overcome with dread, the prince looked to see if anyone had witnessed the murder. Seeing no one, he quickly buried the guard in the sand.

But someone had seen it all. The witness threatened the prince with blackmail, forcing him to flee the country. No more palace, no more riches. He became a fugitive, doomed to wander as a nomad in the barren desert.

For decades the prince wandered, tending sheep. His skin wrinkled and toughened like leather. With the passing of years the prince's sense of destiny faded with the memories of his privileged youth. It seemed the education and training had been wasted on this anonymous desert dweller.

But then in an instant the former prince's life dramatically changed again. One day while walking the desert floor, he detected a burst of color in a plant such as he had never witnessed before. He turned aside and saw a bush that was on fire yet not being consumed, its flames so bright he was forced to shield his eyes and shrink back in stupefied horror. Then from deep within the fire a voice spoke: "Moses, Moses" (Exod. 3:4).

When the prince was able to respond he asked the question—the same question we all ask, "Who are you, God?"

Another man asked the same question centuries later. This man was also a highly educated Jew. Some say he was the most educated Jew in Palestine, one of the most educated men of his day. He was not a fugitive. He was not the hunted. He was the hunter. He had been appointed to seek out those who were fugitives, to find them and cast them into prison.

This man also went into the desert. He, too, saw a light and heard his name spoken: "Saul, Saul, why are you persecuting Me?" (Acts 9:4). Saul, blinded by the brightness of the glory of God, asked, "Who are you, Lord?" (Acts 9:5).

From the day my dad was lowered into the ground I have been asking the same question. Like Moses and Paul, I have begged for an answer: Who are you, God? I know there is a God—we all know that. But that's not nearly enough. I must know who He is. I must know what He is like.

Sure, I know what the creeds say, and the study of theology is my life. Theology is a worthy pursuit because its goal is simply for the individual to know God. But concepts, theories, and abstractions do not excite or ultimately satisfy me. I must know the God who is alive, who is real, who relates to me in my life.

I know that life changes. We decay. We hurt. We die. Nothing in this life is for sure. That's why you and I need a God who is bigger than life, certainly One who is bigger than death. We need a God who cannot be slain, a God who cannot die. Magic won't do. Myths won't work either. This God must be real.

God must be personal, too. We must be able to talk to Him as well as about Him. We need to know His character. That is the purpose of this book. I want to grapple with the majestic character of God. I want to climb the ladder of abstract concepts, but then quickly scurry back down to earth where we live. Where the creeds help we will look at them. More than anything else, we will listen to the Word as we seek to hear God tell us something about Himself. How did He answer Moses, Job, Paul? How does He answer us?

God Answers Moses

When Moses stood quaking in terror before the spectacular bush of fire, not only did he passionately want to know who was speaking to him, but he suddenly had another question of paramount importance. Although he had mused on it at different periods of his life, it now rushed rudely to the foreground of his mind. The question pressed on his temples like a throbbing artery: "Who am I?" (Exod. 3:11).

The two questions do go together. We live in a culture where there is much concern about self-identity. Young people declare that they are searching for themselves, trying to discover who they are. Men read about the dangers of a mid-life crisis. Women struggle to define their role. We seem to be constantly searching for who we are.

The Bible tells us that we are made in the image of God. But can we accurately understand the image until we know the One whose image we bear? The reflection is dim; it is obscure and vague until we discover the source of that reflection. John Calvin once said, "Man never attains a true self-knowledge until he has previously contemplated the face of God and come down after such contemplation to look into himself."

Moses understood that. The two questions he asked were the proper questions: Who is God? Who am I?

When God again spoke to Moses, instead of answering questions, He issued a command. He ordered Moses to remove his shoes. Moses was on sacred turf. He was treading on holy ground:

> "Now therefore, behold, the cry of the children of Israel has come to Me, and I have also seen the oppression with which the Egyptians oppress them. Come now, therefore, and I will send you to Pharaoh that you may bring My people, the children of Israel, out of Egypt."
>
> But Moses said to God, "Who *am* I that I should go to Pharaoh, and that I should bring the children of Israel out of Egypt?" *(Exod. 3:9–11)*

Moses was an old man, well beyond the appropriate years for a mid-life crisis. He wasn't searching for a new self-image. He discovered, however, that God had not stopped by for a casual conversation and a cup of tea. An intrusion by God like this always signifies a call to a weighty mission. God got right to the point and told Moses that he was to liberate the entire Jewish populace from the yoke of Egyptian bondage.

Moses' self-identity was shattered. What was God up to? Moses had been forced to spend decades as an exile from Egypt because he had killed a palace guard in a moment of passionate violence. Now God wanted him to take on Pharaoh himself. Moses was no longer a young man, and the aging process had ravaged his strength. Yet, God was calling him to lead the most spectacular liberation movement in the history of the world.

Moses' self-understanding had never included the idea that he might be the liberator of his people. He had never entertained the idea that he might go personally to the court of Pharaoh and demand the release of the Jews. For Moses to adjust to this idea meant that he had to re-evaluate his own identity. To do that he had to find out who God was.

Moses' dilemma is encountered by all of us. Before we can respond to the divine summons of discipleship or before we can heed the vocation that God gives us, we must first grasp something of the character of the God who is calling us. Our commitment to our mission is only as solid as our understanding of the One who sends us on that mission.

At this point Moses pressed God to at least tell him His name.

Give ear, O LORD, to my prayer;
And attend to the voice of my supplications.
In the day of my trouble I will call upon You,
For You will answer me.
Among the gods there is none like You, O Lord;
Nor are there any works like Your works.
All nations whom You have made
Shall come and worship before You, O Lord,
And shall glorify Your name.
For You are great, and do wondrous things;
You alone are God.
Teach me Your way, O LORD;
I will walk in Your truth;
Unite my heart to fear Your name.
I will praise You, O Lord my God, with all my heart,
And I will glorify Your name forevermore.

Psalm 86:6–12

Then Moses said to God, "Indeed, when I come to the children of Israel and say to them, 'The God of your fathers has sent me to you,' and they say to me, 'What is His name?' what shall I say to them?"

And God said to Moses, "I AM WHO I AM." And He said, "Thus you shall say to the children of Israel, 'I AM has sent me to you.'"

Moreover God said to Moses, "Thus you shall say to the children of Israel: 'The LORD God of your fathers, the God of Abraham, the God of Isaac, and the God of Jacob, has sent me to you. This is My name forever, and this is My memorial to all generations.'" *(Exod. 3:13–15)*

This seemed to be a strange answer to Moses' simple question. God said His name was, "I AM WHO I AM." Is that even an answer? What does it mean? It almost sounds as if God were saying, "Never mind what My name is. My name is none of your business. I am who I am and that's all you need to know. Moses, you can see that I am a very powerful force. But I came here to ask you questions, not to answer yours!"

But such an interpretation doesn't make sense for God goes on to say that this name is to be His memorial. It is to be the name by which He is to be known by all future generations. No, God is not evading Moses' question. He has revealed His name. It is a strange-sounding name, indeed, but it is His real name.

The specific meaning of a name is very significant to the Jews. Often a name is selected that seeks to capture the essence of the person's character. Peter was "the Rock." Isaac means "laughter." Similarly, God's name reveals something profound about Himself, something we must grasp.

As the name Yahweh was uttered by God, there was an explosion of knowledge about God on the Midianite desert. What is so revealing in the words *I AM WHO I AM?*

Who Made You, God?

Chills go up and down my spine when I see the word *aseity*. It's an uncommon word found primarily in theology textbooks. But I love that word because it contains a vital truth of the Christian faith.

Although children do not say *aseity*, every child is concerned about the concept the word represents. The following dialogue takes place in countless homes. It reflects the natural curiosity of children and the simple, direct thinking that occurs in their uninhibited minds. You will recognize it.

"Mommy, who made me?"

"God made you, darling."

"Well, Mommy, who made the sky and the trees?"

"God made the sky and the trees. God made everything."

"Mommy, who made God?"

Oh, oh. Now, what do you say? Who made God? is a natural question for a child. If we teach our children that everything in the world is made from something else, where do we stop this line of reasoning? If everything has a maker, then who makes the maker? If everything has a cause, then who causes the cause? We find clues to the answer in God's curious name for Himself, "I AM WHO I AM."

The "simple" answer (Try explaining this to a child!) is that God does not require a cause. He causes all creatures to be, but He Himself is caused by no one. He makes all things move, but He Himself is moved by nothing.

God exists by His own power. He alone is self-existent. Aseity, meaning "self-existent," is the characteristic that separates Him from all other things. God is the only one who can say, "I am who I am."

Do We Have Anything in Common with God?

The relationship between human beings and the Supreme Being is an arena of great mystery. The obvious answer is that the two beings have *being* in common. But what does it mean 'to be'? We have some idea of what it means to be, because we would find it almost impossible to talk for more than a few seconds without using some form of the verb *to be*. Words like *am*, *are*, *is*, *were*, and *was* are all vital to our patterns of speech.

I remember a song from the forties that had silly lyrics something like this: "Is you is, or is you ain't my baby?" Think of the question: Is you is, or is you ain't? If something is, it is. It can't be "is" and "ain't" at the same time. This is the essence of being. Not one of us can find out if "She loves me or she loves me not" unless we first exist. I must first *be* before I can do anything. I cannot be and not be at the same time.

Whatever Is, Is.

More than two thousand years ago a philosopher by the name of Parmenides declared that "Whatever is, is." You may smile when you hear this quotation, wondering how such a statement could make a man famous. Was Parmenides a prescientific fellow who had a problem with stuttering? The first time I heard Parmenides's famous utterance I laughed. Yet I cannot think of a single philosopher's statement that has snapped into my memory more frequently and caused more consternation than that one.

Another ancient philosopher, Heraclitus, countered Parmenides with his own viewpoint. He declared that "Whatever is, is changing." Heraclitus argued that everything that is, is in a state of flux. He insisted that "You cannot step in the same river twice." What did he mean? Suppose you were to visit the Holy Land and make a pilgrimage to the Jordan River. You might experience a religious awe knowing that you were gazing upon the same river in which Jesus was baptized. You might even dip your toe in the water or fill a jar with a sample of it and treasure it as holy water.

But is this the same river where Jesus was anointed for His earthly ministry? The water of the Jordan is not stagnant. The water is flowing. Like every other river—like Ol' Man River—it just keeps rolling along. If you put one foot in the water, you know that by the time you are able to put the other foot in the river, the river has changed. Even the banks of the river are being changed by erosion.

The plot thickens when we realize that we are changing as well. Between the time the first foot and the second foot submerge in the water, we have changed. If nothing else happens, our bodies are a few seconds older.

Heraclitus understood that what is true of rivers and people is true of everything else in the world. We cannot throw the same rock twice. We cannot smell the same flower twice. We cannot pet the same dog twice. The rock, the flower, the dog all change. Whatever is, is changing.

Here is the problem: If everything is always changing and nothing remains the same, then how can we say that anything 'is'? If everything is always changing then perhaps we cannot speak of 'being' at all but only of 'becoming.' Would our language be more accurate if we spoke of 'human becomings' instead of human beings?

Parmenides would not agree. He would reply that for anything to change it must first be something. Only beings can be changing. If something has no being then it is not. It is nothing. Pure absolute becoming would be nothing. Whatever is changing must be something.

To exist is to participate in being. We do not own being or possess it all by ourselves, but we have the privilege of participating in it. That privilege is granted to us by our Creator who does own being. Being belongs to God. It is part of His nature. He is Being. He is pure Being. God is.

The only way I can *be* is if God makes it possible for me to be. For there to be human beings there must first be a Supreme Being. Without a Supreme Being, nothing could possibly be.

To be involves a kind of power, a kind of ability. You and I are aware of different abilities—the ability to paint, the ability to swim, the ability to fly. They require a certain kind of power for the activity to take place. But the most important ability we need is the ability to exist. Without that ability, that power, all other abilities would be meaningless.

The grand difference between a human being and a Supreme Being is precisely this: Apart from God I cannot exist; apart from me God does exist. God does not need me in order for Him to be. I do need God in order for me to be. This is the difference between what we call self-existent Being and dependent being.

Every year I must file a federal income tax return on which I list my "dependents." The word *dependent* refers to those persons who, for some reason, depend upon me for their livelihood. Yet all of us are dependent, and human life is far more fragile than we often like to admit.

My son-in-law had an experience at age twenty-seven, the specifics of which he does not remember but his friends and family will never forget. He went to a gymnasium to play basketball. Less than sixty seconds after the opening tip-off, he fell to the floor unconscious. His heart stopped beating and he ceased breathing. For five minutes he was dead from acute cardiac arrest. To his good fortune fully-trained paramedics arrived on the scene and were able to revive his heart and breathing. He survived this near-fatal heart attack.

My son-in-law experienced the grim reality of one heartbeat away from death. He learned what we all must face, that we do not have the power of being within ourselves. We are dependent. We are fragile. We cannot live without air, without water, without food.

No human being has the power of being within himself. Life is lived between two hospitals. We need a support system from birth to death to sustain life. As the Scripture states, "life is grass" (Isa. 40:6–8). We are like flowers that bloom and then wither and fade. This is how we differ from God. God does not wither. God does not fade. God is not fragile. The very word *existence* is not quite accurate for Him.

Did God Make Himself?

Once again we must face the child's question: "Who made God?" I once heard a dialogue between two children about this matter. The four-year-old asked the question; and the five-year-old answered: "God made Hisself!"

That sounds cute, but cute or not, when I heard this heresy I had to jump into the debate. I challenged the five-year-old's answer whereupon he adjusted it without batting an eyelash. His new answer was "Jesus made God." When I asked who made Jesus, the reply was equally facile: "God made Jesus." With the reply came a Cheshire-cat smile, indicating that nothing could possibly be simpler.

To say that God made Himself is to say that God is self-created. The concept of a self-created God involves a thinly disguised contradiction. What would have to happen for something to create itself? To create itself, something, even God, would have to *be* before it is. It would have to exist and not exist at the same time. To create itself it would have to pull itself into existence before it had anything to pull with. The very concept of self-creation is irrational. God could not have "made Himself."

On the other hand, to say that God is self-existent does not involve any contradiction and is not irrational. To say that God is self-existent simply means that there was no time when God started to exist. He has always been. He is eternal. He has no beginning and no end. Nothing caused God to come into existence. God did not make Himself. He made us. In a word, God is not a creature. He is not dependent. He is not derived. He is not fragile. Rather, God is the Creator. He is independent, self-sufficient, and secure. God, and God alone, has the power of being within Himself. He is who He is. "I AM WHO I AM." That God is self-existent means that he is unique. He alone is the source of all being. He alone has the power of being. He alone is eternal. He alone is supreme. But how does all of this relate to the biblical portrait of God?

So What?

Any time that we explore concepts in theology we are brought sooner or later to the obvious question, So what? What difference does it make to my life that God is self-existent?

When I stood at the side of my father's grave I was haunted by the finality of death. I was staring into the pit of the end of being. My father was dead. He no longer was. His body was all that was left and it, too, was already in the process of decay. No more Saturday morning hugs. No more dragging his ravaged body to the dining room table. All that was left to do was to chisel the dates of his birth and his death onto stone. The power of being had left this human being. Life had departed. Only an inert, unconscious, unresponsive corpse was left. Forever.

Forever? Maybe not. On that day of burial I had never heard of the prophet Ezekiel. Later I read the prophet's story. He also had attended a funeral. In his mind he was attending not the funeral of a person but the funeral of a nation. He was an eyewitness, a participant of the Babylonian captivity of Israel. He lived out the exile of God's people. His was an exodus in reverse; he marched backward out of the Promised Land in an ignominious defeat. This time no pillar of fire or cloud led the children of God. Instead, a cloud of doom hung over their heads.

The glory of Israel was finished. Once more they were in bondage, their spiritual heritage dead. Their groans rose toward heaven.

God spoke to Ezekiel. He carried him off in the palm of His hand and put him down in a mass graveyard, a valley of dry bones. In this place of death were no rotting corpses. The vultures had already plucked the bones clean. The bones had been bleached white by the sun. They were brittle and stacked in a chaotic pile.

The place was deserted—even the vultures had departed. Here was total death, an absolute void of being.

On this site God questioned Ezekiel, "Son of man, can these bones live again?"

"Lord God, you know," Ezekiel replied.

Was the prophet hedging his answer with a clever evasion? Did he mean, "I don't have any idea. You are the only one who can answer the question." Or was Ezekiel's answer a response of mighty faith? Was he saying, "You know it! I'm sure that if You give the word, even these arid bones can come to life."

God then answered His own question, commanding Ezekiel to preach to this "congregation." A preacher would feel rather self-conscious practicing his oratory in a bone yard. But Ezekiel understood his mission. He was not responsible for the response; his task was to preach. God told him to call upon the four winds to blow upon this lifeless mass, so Ezekiel spoke to the bones:

> So I prophesied as I was commanded; and as I prophesied, there was a noise, and suddenly a rattling; and the bones came together, bone to bone.
> Indeed, as I looked, the sinews and the flesh came upon them, and the skin covered them over; but there was no breath in them. *(Ezek. 37:7–8)*

A skeletal dance erupted before the prophet's eyes. Bones came together, knitting to each other in perfect form. Flesh, muscle, and tissue covered the bones, but still there was no life. Then Ezekiel called the wind, voicing the command of God:

> "Come from the four winds, O breath, and breathe on these slain, that they may live."
> So I prophesied as He commanded me, and breath came into them, and they lived, and stood upon their feet, an exceedingly great army. *(Ezek. 37:9–10)*

In an instant there stood an army of living persons in the valley. The bones were no longer dry. The God of being brought life out of death.

This was the vision of Ezekiel. The vision of God bringing life out of death must be the vision of the people of God in every age. It is the vision I missed by my father's grave. It is a meaningful response to our So what? question.

Our self-existent God also appeared in another vision, a vision given to Saint John on the island of Patmos: "'I am the Alpha and the Omega, *the* Beginning and *the* End,' says the Lord, 'who is and who was and who is to come, the Almighty'" (Rev. 1:8).

The Lord God revealed Himself here as the Alpha and the Omega. That is, He encompasses the beginning of the alphabet and the end of it. He is the "A to Z." He is the eternal One who has the power of being in Himself. This self-description of the Lord God is also used to describe the exalted Christ:

Then I turned to see the voice that spoke with me. And having turned I saw seven golden lampstands, and in the midst of the seven lampstands One like the Son of Man, clothed with a garment down to the feet and girded about the chest with a golden band. His head and His hair were white like wool, as white as snow, and His eyes like a flame of fire; his feet were like fine brass, as if refined in a furnace, and His voice as the sound of many waters; He had in His right hand seven stars, out of His mouth went a sharp two-edged sword, and His countenance was like the sun shining in its strength. And when I saw Him, I fell at His feet as dead. But He laid his right hand on me, saying to me, "Do not be afraid; I am the First and the Last. I am He who lives, and was dead, and behold, I am alive forevermore. Amen. And I have the keys of Hades and of Death." *(Rev. 1:12–18)*

Here the title reserved for God is transferred to Christ who is now called the Alpha and the Omega. Jesus said to John, "Do not be afraid." Fear is no longer relevant because John is with the One who has the power of being.

Our deepest fears flow out of our fragility. I am afraid of cancer. I am afraid of flying. I am afraid of pain. I am afraid of the valley of the shadow of death. These fears are relieved when I realize that Jesus holds the keys to death and to Hades. The threat of death is the threat of non-being. Jesus died. When He strode forth from the tomb, He carried with Him the keys of death. Like a prisoner who escapes from his cell and locks the sheriff up, making him captive in his own jail, so Christ emerged from the grave with the keys to the jail in His hand.

Jesus is a Savior with power, ultimate power, and He holds the power of being in His hand. His words, "Do not be afraid," are not empty words. I have nothing to fear from death. My Savior holds the keys. This is a concrete, meaningful answer to our So what? question.

Another important matter related to God's self-existence is found in Paul's letter to the Romans: "(as it is written, *'I have made you a father of many nations')* in the presence of Him whom he believed, even God, who gives life to the dead and calls those things which do not exist as though they did" (Rom. 4:17).

O LORD, our Lord,
How excellent is Your name in all the earth,
You who set Your glory above the heavens!
Out of the mouth of babes and infants
You have ordained strength,
Because of Your enemies,
That You may silence the enemy and the avenger.
When I consider Your heavens, the work of Your fingers,
The moon and the stars, which You have ordained,
What is man that You are mindful of him,
And the son of man that You visit him?
For You have made him a little lower than the angels,
And You have crowned him with glory and honor.
You have made him to have dominion over the works of Your hands;
You have put all things under his feet,
All sheep and oxen—
Even the beasts of the field,
The birds of the air,
And the fish of the sea
That pass through the paths of the seas.
O LORD, our Lord,
How excellent is Your name in all the earth!

Psalm 8

In this passage Paul discussed saving faith. He called attention to the One in whom we must put our trust. The God we believe in and dedicate our lives to (1) brings life out of death and (2) brings into being that which does not exist. These two ideas summarize the supreme power of God. He can give breath to the lifeless corpse and He can make something out of nothing.

We are awed by the grand difference between human beings and the Supreme Being: No human being can bring life out of death; no human being can make something out of nothing. So what? What difference does this make? All the difference in the world—the difference between life and death, between being and non-being, between something and nothing, between a futile faith and a vital faith.

There is one other crucial passage in the book of Acts that has bearing on our being and the Being of God: "God, who made the world and everything in it, since He is Lord of heaven and earth, does not dwell in temples made with hands. Nor is He worshiped with men's hands, as though He needed anything, since He gives to all life, breath, and all things. . . . for in Him we live and move and have our being" (Acts 17:24–28).

In the history of philosophy and science three great puzzles, three mysteries have baffled the greatest of minds: life, motion, and being. No one has yet unraveled the mystery of life. The concept of motion remains elusive. The idea of being occupies both the philosopher and the scientist. Yet, in these verses in Acts a clue to solving the mystery of all three concepts is found. It is in *God* that we *live* and *move* and *have* our *being*.

In Him we *live*. The power supply for life is God. He is the author and the source of all life. His power to call forth life is what qualifies Him alone to be the Creator. We understand the cry of the Psalmist, "It is He who has made us and not we ourselves" (Ps. 100:3).

In Him we *move*. Motion finds its ultimate impetus in God. Without Him everything would be stagnant, immobile, static, inert—*lifeless*. That which moves, that which is dynamic finds its power in God. We move because He moves.

In Him we have our *being*. It is because of His self-existence that we can exist at all. You and I exist in His power and by His power. We *are* because He *is*.

25

I Want to Find You, God.

When I was a college student, one of my electives was a course in hymnology. I found it fascinating to study the development and theory of Christian hymns. Our professor was an accomplished organist, a virtuoso whose hands and feet flew over the multiple keyboards, pedals, and stops on the great pipe organ. He embodied the role of the artistic, fussy musician. His spirit soared with the strains of the classics. He adored the music of Mendelssohn, Handel, and Bach.

But the professor's eyebrows arched and his spirit sank at the dreadful tones of "lowbrow" church music. He had contempt for hymns that "sounded as if they were written in saloons or composed for roller rinks." His annoyance turned to full digust for one song in particular, the old-fashioned hymn "In the Garden." He shuddered at lyrics of dew and roses. To him the song sounded like a perfect selection for a roller rink's "all skate."

Since I was a typical college student—always looking for a break in the routine—I could not resist the temptation to torment our professor's musical sensibilities. The class met in a studio that contained a piano. One morning I made sure that I arrived early and positioned myself at the keyboard. A fellow student was posted as a lookout near the door. As soon as the professor came within earshot, the lookout signaled, and with a revival-night flourish, I began to play "In the Garden." The poor professor, a grimace etched in his face, entered his classroom to the sound of his most-hated hymn.

This "game" became an instant tradition, making the professor at first, apoplectic, but after awhile, amused by our sophomoric fun.

Even now I, too, find the music and lyrics of "In the Garden" too saccharine for my tastes. Yet I am haunted by one refrain in that song—"He walks with me and He talks with me and He tells me I am His own."

Is there anyone of us who claims Jesus as Lord whose heart does not beat with a passion to hear the voice of God? Who wouldn't sell every possession to be able to walk in a garden alone with Jesus? To talk to Him? What would you give to hear Christ say audibly to you, "You are mine. You belong to me, now and forever"?

The disciples walking the road to Emmaus twenty centuries ago had this experience. Christ joined them unexpectedly. He concealed His identity so that they didn't recognize the "stranger" at their side. These men were not in a garden. There were no roses covered with dew. But they walked and talked with the risen Christ. What was their experience like? When their eyes were finally opened and they recognized Jesus, He suddenly vanished. Here is their "on the scene" reaction: "And they said to one another, 'Did not our heart burn within us while He talked with us on the road, and while He opened the Scriptures to us?'" (Luke 24:32).

"Hearts burning within us"—that is the normal human reaction to the immediate presence of Christ. My heart would be scorched to a cinder if I could hear His voice. My soul would explode in joy if I could walk with Him and talk to Him. I would travel the world to find a garden where He was visibly present.

But the truth is that I can't see God. I can't even see His shadow. He leaves no footprints in the sand, no fingerprints on the doorknob, no lingering aroma of after-shave in the breeze. He is invisible because He is immaterial.

And the Incarnate Son who once was visible to human eyes has left this planet in His bodily presence. Though Jesus remains with us in His divine nature, that nature is invisible.

God's invisibility confounds me. We human beings are sensual creatures. We respond to what we can see, hear, and touch. Like Thomas, the Doubting One, we long to place our fingers into Jesus' wounds and verify with our senses that it is really He.

I have often wondered how different my life would be if I could see the invisible God. It is hard to love and to serve someone I have never seen. Unfortunately, the axiom "out of sight, out of mind" seems to be painfully true with our faith. Is it possible that the extraordinary faith and power of the early Christian Church were related to the fact that those people had seen the risen Christ? They had been eyewitnesses to a "God with skin on."

I have never seen God, with or without skin. I have never heard His voice. I've met people who have said that God spoke to them. When I have probed their statement, however, invariably I find they "heard" the voice of God in the Bible or in the silent chamber of their heart. Once or twice people have insisted to me that they heard the audible voice of God. I do not believe this. I am sure they are sincere and think they heard the actual voice of God, but I believe the voice of God is silent today. We can read His words in the Bible, but apart from Scripture, we hear no words from God.

Because God is silent and invisible, we tend to think He is absent from us. When we can't "feel" His presence with the accompanying tingle on the back of the neck and the chill along the spinal cord, we tend to think He is absent. Our experience is more of the divine absence than of the divine presence.

Our generation has faced a crisis of faith about the nearness of God. Modern man is still "waiting for Godot." The theologians, not the secular philosophers, announced the death of God. The mood of our culture reflects a sense of abandonment. God seems nowhere to be found.

A man named Anthony Flew composed a now-famous parable to illustrate modern man's dilemma about speaking of God. He told the story of two explorers who penetrated a remote area of African jungle. Far from civilization they stumbled upon a clearing that contained a marvelous garden with perfectly symmetrical rows of plants. No weeds were growing, and the garden appeared fully cultivated.

Certain that there must be a gardener nearby, the explorers set up camp and waited for him to appear. The gardener never came. The first explorer suggested that they move along, but the second explorer protested, suggesting that perhaps the gardener was invisible. Maybe the gardener was slipping into the garden during the night. So the explorers set up a wire fence around the garden and hung bells from it that would ring in the event that the invisible gardener came to tend the garden.

During that night and subsequent nights the bells never rang. The first explorer now insisted that they move on. The second explorer still wanted to stay and wait for the gardener. He said to his comrade, "Maybe the gardener is not only invisible but immaterial as well." To this the first explorer replied, "What is the difference between an invisible, immaterial gardener and no gardener at all?"

Flew went on to declare that modern man has experienced the death of God in his language: "God has died the death of a thousand qualifications." The point is that people who believe in an invisible God have so defined God that it is impossible to disprove Him. Scientific tests cannot be done on God; He cannot be examined under a microscope.

What is the difference between an invisible and immaterial God and no God at all? The implied answer in Flew's parable is that there is no difference. But in fact, the difference screams out at us. *The difference is the garden.* The presence of an intelligently cultivated and maintained garden is something we would not find without a gardener. The garden gives testimony to both the presence and the power of the gardener. There is nothing irrational or unreasonable about the idea of an invisible, immaterial gardener. There is something terribly problematic about a perfectly symmetrical, weedless garden growing without a gardener in the middle of the jungle.

Jesus spoke to Nicodemus about the power and the presence of the Holy Spirit. He spoke of the mysterious way in which the Spirit works. He is like the wind that blows where it wants to. We can't see it, but we can feel it. His presence is known *by His effects.* The effects are real because the power and the presence are real. The difference between an invisible, immaterial God and no God at all is the difference between the divine presence and the divine absence, between divine power and divine impotence, between ultimate joy and ultimate despair.

What Is Infinity?

God is a spirit. His presence is not limited to a remote garden in Africa. His presence is boundless. God is not merely a spirit; He is an infinite spirit.

As soon as we say that God is an infinite spirit we enter a difficult arena of thought. The very concept of 'infinity' tends to overwhelm us. We are finite. As finite beings we cannot fully fathom the infinite. The idea is too much for our grasp.

Even though we cannot grasp the infinite, we know that some idea of the infinite is necessary to our thinking. We need some kind of working definition of infinity.

A math professor once was lecturing on the concept of infinity. Approaching the subject in abstract terms, he never quite landed on a definition. Finally a frustrated student blurted out, "Professor, I still don't understand what you mean by 'infinite.'" The professor stopped lecturing, took a piece of chalk, and began to draw a line on the extreme left side of the blackboard at the front of the room. He walked the line all the way across the front blackboard and then continued drawing the line on the wall. He drew around the corner, across the face of the classroom door, to the back wall, and all the way around the room until he finished by connecting the line to his original starting point. He dropped the chalk in the tray, brushed his hands together, and said, "There is infinity."

Drawing a line that had no end was how the math teacher tried to illustrate infinity. A simple circle would have done as well. An infinite line has no end. Here the term *infinite* is defined by saying what it is not: It is not finite. A finite line has an end to it; an infinite line has no end to it.

But what if the math teacher had continued his demonstration by going to the blackboard and drawing a second line around the room three inches below the first one? Now he would have had two "infinite" lines. It is therefore possible to have more than one infinite line, because the line is infinite in only one direction.

But how many infinite *beings* can there be? If we mean that an infinite being encompasses all being in every direction, of every kind, and in every dimension, then obviously there can be only one such being. If this being is everywhere and everything at once, does that mean that no other being could exist?

This is one of the more excruciating problems encountered in Christian thought. We say easily that God is infinite but quickly retreat from the difficulties that surround this idea.

Part of the solution to this dilemma is found in the very first sentence of the Bible: "In the beginning God created the heavens and the earth" (Gen. 1:1). In this verse we note a distinction between God and the world He created. This distinction is maintained throughout the whole of Scripture. The Creator is not the creation, and the creation is not the Creator. To obscure this difference or to confuse the two is to be guilty of idolatry.

But if God is an infinite spirit, if He has infinite being, how can we distinguish between God and the world? In a word, this is the challenge of pantheism, which has been so tempting an "answer" to so many.

The Lure of Pantheism

What is pantheism? The term is made up of a prefix *pan* and a root *theos*. *Pan* means "all." Pan American airlines was so named because it flew to all of the Americas. *Theos* is the Greek word for "God." Hence we see that the word *pantheism* means literally "all of God."

The common denominator of the various forms of pantheism is the idea that the being, the essence, of all things is the being of God. The pantheist says that the universe is essentially God and that God is essentially the universe. All is God and God is all.

Pantheism is filled with many dangers. On the one hand, it is a form of atheism. Strangely, pantheism appears to acknowledge the existence of God. If everything is God, either there is a whole lot of God or there are many, many gods. If we think about it, however, we will conclude that if everything is God, then nothing is God. If the whole world is God, then the term *God* no longer points to something or someone distinctive. If there is no essential difference between God and the world, then the very word *God* becomes excess baggage and only serves to confuse matters.

If all is God then R. C. Sproul is God or at least a part of God. If pantheism is correct, then the promise Satan made to Eve has been kept: "You shall be as gods" (Gen. 3:5). Pantheism can be very flattering to human beings.

I was born a creature. In conversion to Christ I remained a creature even though I became indwelt by the Holy Spirit. I am in Christ and He is in me. But I am not Christ and Christ is not R. C. Sproul. Nor will R. C. Sproul ever become Christ. Christ and I have a *type* of union but not a union where the identities of Jesus Christ and R. C. Sproul are obscured or confused.

There is a genuine form of Christian mysticism. But the goal of Christian mysticism is not union with God but *communion*. We seek to rise no higher than the blessed heights of mystic sweet communion with God. In fact, there is no time I am more acutely aware that I am not God than when I am in communion with God.

God's Omnipresence

Because God is an infinite spirit, He can be omnipresent. He is everywhere present. God fills all space. The universe is replete with His divine presence.

Here we see the crucial problem. If God fills all space, if His being permeates everything that is, how can there be something besides God? Why do we not say that He is everything?

Let's look at the problem another way. There is a tree in my back yard. God created that tree and He sustains it. It cannot continue to exist for five seconds without the sustaining power of being that resides in God and in God alone. God's infinite being fills that tree. Every drop of sap is permeated by God. The bark of the tree is filled with the presence of God. The question is, Where does God end and the tree start? If no part of the tree is not God, then we must bow to the logic of pantheism and say that the tree is God or is at least a part of God.

If there is something that is apart from the being of God, where does that "something" begin and the being of God end? And, if there is some place where God's being ends, how and why do we speak of God's infinity?

When we speak like this and describe God with physical terms, we immediately are handicapped. When we say "a place where," we are using language that doesn't apply to an infinite spirit. What we mean by this language is that there must be some kind of "boundary" between the being of God and the being of the world. This boundary, however, is not a "Checkpoint Charley" with patrolling guards.

The boundary between God and the world is a boundary of being. The being of this world is a lower order of being than the being of God. It is lower in that it does not contain within itself the power of being. The power of self-existence is lacking. Creaturely being is sustained and supported moment to moment by the power of God's being but is not itself God's being.

Creaturely being is neither an extension of God's being nor a mode of God's being. We must avoid both of these concepts: 1) The world is the same essence as God—an extension of God— as the rays of the sun are the same essence as the sun but not the sun. 2) The world is a lower level or mode of the being of God—that is, various levels of God exist—beginning with pure God and descending to spirit, mind, matter, and non-being—which become less pure as the levels approach matter.

The being of God pervades the world and holds it together. How this happens is as mysterious as the how of creation. We must rest in our understanding that the how of creation and the sustaining of creation are found in the self-existing power of the Creator. There is nothing irrational about this mystery; it violates no law of logic. Its full meaning, however, escapes our understanding.

To say that God is an infinite being and yet deny that God is all being is not a contradiction because we are not talking about the same kind of being. We have already seen the illustration of the infinite line. We understand that there can be more than one infinite line. To escape the infinite line of a circle, to stop going around and around we need to move off the plane of the line. The move is a dimensional move.

We are creatures who live in three dimensions. We understand one dimension and two dimensions and so on. But we have no experience of a fifth or sixth dimension, if there are such dimensions to reality. Higher dimensional mathematics hints at these higher levels of reality, but we have no experience of them.

The Supernatural Realm

Christianity is a supernatural religion. There have been numerous attempts to desupernaturalize Christianity to accommodate it to unbelief, but the historic Christian faith is unabashedly supernatural. Those who seek to naturalize it and retain the name "Christian" are being dishonest.

A supernaturalist affirms that there exists a higher plane of reality than the plane upon which we live our daily lives. This other reality is the spiritual realm.

Although it is largely invisible to us, we know a natural invisible realm surrounds us. These natural entities are so small that they are visible to us only via sophisticated scientific instruments. Although these microscopic and submicroscopic natural entities are not spiritual beings, their power can destroy us.

When someone with a cold sneezes, we want to duck. We know that the sneeze has just sprayed invisible germs into the air, and we want to escape their contagious assault. We know also that there are other invisible microbodies that can afflict us with diseases far worse than the common cold. But this other invisible realm is still a part of nature. When we speak of supernature we are speaking of another dimension altogether.

The normal barrier between nature and supernature was revealed in the experience of Israel's prophet Elisha. In his time the king of Syria was waging war against Israel. Every time the king of Syria made his battle plans and set his marching routes, God revealed this information to Elisha. Elisha then communicated this "classified information" to the king of Israel, who escaped the Syrian attacks.

At first the Syrian king was convinced that there was a security leak in his own army. Was a Jewish "mole" deeply buried among his own trusted men? Eventually the king learned Elisha was the one telling the king's secrets to the king of Israel.

Angered by this knowledge the Syrian king set out to capture Elisha. He learned that Elisha was living in a place named Dothan. Second Kings tells what happened:

> Therefore he sent horses and chariots and a great army there, and they came by night and surrounded the city. And when the servant of the man [Elisha] of God arose early and went out, there was an army, surrounding the city with horses and chariots. And his servant said to him, "Alas, my master! What shall we do?"
>
> So he answered, "Do not fear, for those who are with us are more than those who are with them."
>
> And Elisha prayed, and said, "LORD, I pray, open his eyes that he may see." Then the LORD opened the eyes of the young man, and he saw. And behold, the mountain was full of horses and chariots of fire all around Elisha.
>
> *(2 Kings 6:14–17)*

This servant had a definite conflict of faith. Should he believe what his eyes were telling him or what his master, Elisha, was telling him? When Elisha told him that those who were with him outnumbered the army of the Syrians, the servant must have wondered about Elisha's sanity. But Elisha was speaking of supernatural things whereas his servant was stuck with a natural perspective. The two men were speaking on two different planes. Theirs was a dimensional misunderstanding.

Rather than argue the point, Elisha prayed that God would let his servant get a glimpse through the veil. He asked God to let the invisible become visible. He requested a dimensional breakthrough.

God granted the request. For a fleeting moment the veil was lifted. The servant peeked across the border and beheld "chariots of fire." This sort of dimensional barrier exists between the being of God and the being of the world, between the natural and the supernatural.

Consider another illustration. Have you looked at yourself in a mirror recently? Before you answer the question you may want to go back and read the question again. I hope you answered no. Why? I did not ask you if you had looked at your *image* or your *reflection* in the mirror recently. I asked if you had looked at *yourself*.

If you failed this "pop quiz" don't feel bad—this is the way we normally talk. We speak of looking at ourselves in the mirror. But is that really us in there? When I stand before a mirror, is my being suddenly changed from three dimensions into two dimensions that then crawl into the mirror? Is that really me in there? It does look like me, but it is just my mirror image. All I see in the mirror is a flat, two dimensional reflection. The same effect is found in photographs.

No camera can capture my soul. No mirror can even give me an accurate picture of what I look like. My image is flip-flopped around so that the image I see is not what I really look like. For example, I have a mole on the right side of my face. When I look in the mirror I see a man with a mole on the left side of his face. That man is not me.

Passage to Another Dimension

Why should we assume that the only dimensions of reality that exist are the dimensions we are accustomed to? Even natural reason by analogy suggests the unlikelihood that, in the vast complexity of the universe, we are the pinnacle of life. On our own small planet we see all sorts of living things— beings that live in the water, beings that live in the arctic snow, beings that fly through the air, beings that live in holes in the ground, and beings that live in condominiums in Fort Lauderdale. Are the latter the last and highest order of being in the entire universe? The humanist thinks so, but his assumption is as arrogant as it is gratuitous.

The Bible tells us that God is an infinite spirit who is present everywhere. Where is He? He is right here. Right now. The barrier between God and us is neither space nor time, neither the here nor the now. God is in the here and the now. The barrier is dimensional. To step into His immediate presence would be to step not into the future or into the sky but through a dimensional veil. He is here with us and all that He is is with us.

Most of us as children learned the Twenty-third Psalm. Many times since my childhood the comforting words of that Psalm have raced across the screen of my mind. The verse I love the most is "Yea, though I walk through the valley of the shadow of death, I will fear no evil, for Thou art with me" (v. 4).

"For Thou art with me." Here is where the rubber of my faith hits the road. Here is where I cry, "Lord, I believe, help Thou my unbelief."

God promises you and me His presence. I don't always feel His presence. But God's promises do not depend upon my feelings; they rest upon His integrity. I may fail in my promises, but He does not break His. My doubts about His presence insult His integrity. Because I cannot see Him or feel Him, I begin to question His Word. To live by faith, on the other hand, is to live by trust. This means far more than believing in God; it means believing God.

Many things about this world frighten me. I have no desire to be tortured. I have no desire to be maimed in a car wreck. I have no desire to suffer with cancer. Who would want to experience any of these troubles? But I would be less anxious if I knew for sure that if any of these things befell me God would be with me every second. Of course, He *has* promised that He will certainly be with me. But my faith still wavers. I struggle with the dimensional barrier.

The Immensity of God: He Is Fully Present Everywhere

When we speak of the infinity of God and of His omnipresence, we usually add to this the idea of God's immensity. The word is a disputed one in theology and can be misleading. Typically, *immensity* means something is extremely large. If we are not careful we may think that the way God is present is by being very large. Is part of God in Los Angeles and another part of Him in New York? God's omnipresence is not like that. Another word, *ubiquity*, which is usually used as a synonym for omnipresence, more clearly expresses what we mean by the immensity of God. Its literal meaning is "equal-whereness." The idea is this: Wherever God is present, He is *fully present*—that is, He is present in the fullness of His being. When believers live in Los Angeles, they enjoy the fullness of the presence of God. At the same time, believers in New York also enjoy the fullness of the presence of God. He can be everywhere, equally present.

Violinist J. Oliver Buswell related an illustration his father gave from the pulpit when Buswell was a child. His father said, "Everyone in the world is immediately in the presence of God, just as everyone in this room is immediately in my presence." God is always and everywhere at hand.

The practical benefits of God's infinity are great and marvelous. God is able to be present with you and me. He also *wants* to be present. We can be sure of His undivided attention. I never have to stand in line to meet with God. I do not need a prior appointment. Because He is infinite in His being, and because wherever He is, He is there in His fullness, I can have His undivided attention at exactly the same moment you enjoy His undivided attention. He can walk with you and talk with you in your garden at the same time He is present with me in my garden. There is another side, however, to this wonderful characteristic of God.

Good News and Bad News

For those who have tasted the sweetness of the forgiveness of and reconciliation with God, His ubiquity is good news. But for those who remain hostile and estranged from God, His omnipresence is very bad news. There is nothing a fugitive wants to hear less than that his pursuer is everywhere. There is no place to hide from an infinite spirit. His eye is on the sparrow when it falls. His eye is also on the thief when he steals.

There are those who hate God's presence because they cannot stand His gaze. But for those who love His appearing, the presence of God is like soothing music. When Jesus told His disciples that in a short time He would leave the earth, He made a marvelous promise: "Lo, I am with you always, even to the end of the age" (Matt. 28:20). Jesus could make this promise because He is God incarnate. One historic creed states it this way: "Touching His human nature, Jesus is no longer present with us; touching His divine nature, He is never absent from us." Because the divine nature of Christ has

39

all the attributes of the Godhead, Jesus could make the solemn promise, "I will be with you always."

In our garden we can see the dew. We can see the roses. But we can't see Him, so His presence seems less real than the dew and the roses. In a real sense, however, His presence is greater, more powerful than the dew and the roses. As the morning sun rises to full strength, the dew evaporates, but God's presence remains. As the days pass the roses wilt and fade, but the infinite God abides. He does not wilt. He does not fade. He is present with us. He walks in our garden. Always and everywhere.

O Lord, You have searched me and known me.
You know my sitting down and my rising up;
You understand my thought afar off.
You comprehend my path and my lying down,
And are acquainted with all my ways.

. . . .

You have hedged me behind and before,
And laid Your hand upon me.
Such knowledge is too wonderful for me;
It is high, I cannot attain it.
Where can I go from Your Spirit?
Or where can I flee from Your presence?
If I ascend into heaven, You are there;
If I make my bed in hell, behold, You are there.
If I take the wings of the morning,
And dwell in the uttermost parts of the sea,
Even there Your hand shall lead me,
And Your right hand shall hold me.
If I say, "Surely the darkness shall fall on me,"
Even the night shall be light about me;
Indeed, the darkness shall not hide from You,
But the night shines as the day;
The darkness and the light are both alike to You.

. . . .

When I awake, I am still with You.

Psalm 139:1–3, 5–12, 18

I Can't See You, God.

It was 1964—my senior year of seminary. I was seated comfortably in a theology class one morning when the professor announced that today the class would play his "learning game." My stomach fluttered. Others shifted in their chairs. I could almost smell the anxiety in the room. The professor's "game" followed the teaching method made famous by Socrates where, after a difficult question was posed, the students were engaged in rigorous dialogue on the issue. The professor was brilliant and in debate he often made us feel like our heads were full of sawdust.

This time the professor had decided to pose as a Mormon. He was insisting, as orthodox Mormonism does, that God has a physical body. Our task was to prove to our "Mormon" professor that God does not have a body.

After introducing the topic, the professor paused and peered at the class. We sat motionless with our eyes averted while his gaze—roaming the room, up and down the aisle—probed like a grim searchlight in a prison camp for any poor soul attempting to escape. Finally, the professor fixed his eyes on one unfortunate student, his first victim for the debate.

"Mr. Sproul, how do we know that God does not have a body?"

I almost swallowed my Adam's apple. Forcing air into my vocal chords, I feebly squeaked Jesus' words in John 4:24: "God is Spirit, and those who worship Him must worship Him in spirit and in truth." I said, "The Scriptures clearly declared here that God is a spirit and not a body."

"No," the professor answered. "You are saying more than the Scriptures say. The Bible says that God is a spirit but it does not add 'and not a body.' Just because something is a spirit does not mean it cannot also have a body."

My mind was spinning. My face had turned red. I could force no words from my mouth. "Mr. Sproul, do you have a body?" the professor said, pressing his point.

"Of course," I replied, my voice still wavering.

"Are you not also a spirit? When God created man He breathed into man the breath of life, and, the Scripture says, 'man became a living soul.' There we find clear biblical teaching that something can be both body and soul. If man is a spirit and has a body, why can't God also be a spirit and have a body as well? The Bible repeatedly describes God in physical terms. He 'comes and goes.' He has a face, arms, and legs. He creates man in His own image. How can something that has no body have an image?"

Regaining some self-control, I protested. "But, professor, that is precisely the point of Jesus' words to the woman of Sychar. The woman had inquired about the proper place to worship God. The whole discussion centered on God's location. What Jesus was teaching was that God cannot be confined to a particular location because God is a spirit. Bodies are confined to particular places, but spirits are not. So the issue Jesus was discussing was not if God was spirit *and* body but if God has a body at all."

"No, no, no, Mr. Sproul. That will never do," the professor insisted. "The point Jesus was making was that God's body and spirit were not so small as to be confined merely to Jerusalem or to Mount Gerizim. Rather God's spirit-body is so large that it encompasses both places at the same time."

With that retort I sank back into my chair and abandoned any further debate. The rest of the class fought in vain for orthodox Christianity until, one by one, every student surrendered. The professor convinced us at every turn that the Bible does not deny that God has a body. Exhausted, we wondered if our only choice was to become Mormons. Yet, we all knew the professor did not believe the claim he had so convincingly made.

As the end of the class neared we begged the professor, "Please, tell us the answer. What should we say to the Mormon who insists that God has a body?"

With a satisfied smile the professor replied, "The most crucial biblical text to refute the crass idea that God has a physical body is found in John 4. Jesus declared to the Samaritan woman that God is a spirit."

My arm shot into the air, "Wait a minute! That's what I said! But you said all that stuff about man's being a spirit and a body. And when I tried to show that Jesus was debating an issue of location you said, 'No, no, no, Mr. Sproul, that will never do.'"

"That's right, I did say that. But, Mr. Sproul, what kind of an argument is 'No, no, no. That will never do'? I kept talking when you had me on the ropes, and you simply let me squirm away. Because I didn't surrender to your argument you abandoned it."

The class erupted with laughter, but as we left the room, I realized I had learned *two* lessons. The first was about God's spirituality, and the second was about how human beings debate issues.

Of course, the first point is the more important: God *is* a spirit. But what does that really mean? The discussion between Jesus and the Samaritan woman does provide part of the answer.

The woman Jesus met by the well perceived that Jesus was a prophet, someone who could answer thorny theological questions. What would you have asked Jesus if given the same opportunity? Here's what the Samaritan woman wanted to find out:

"Our fathers worshiped on this mountain, and you Jews say that in Jerusalem is the place where one ought to worship." Jesus said to her, "Woman, believe Me, the hour is coming when you will neither on this mountain, nor in Jerusalem, worship the Father. You worship what you do not know; we know what we worship; for salvation is of the Jews. But the hour is coming, and now is, when the true worshipers will worship the Father in spirit and truth; for the Father is seeking such to worship Him. God is Spirit, and those who worship Him must worship in spirit and truth." *(John 4:20–24)*

The woman's question grew out of an ongoing debate between the Samaritans and the Jews about the true center of worship. We could easily miss one of Jesus' key points here by leaping to the conclusion that Jesus was saying, "A pox on both your houses. You are both wrong. It doesn't matter where you worship God, but how you worship Him."

That's not it. Jesus was making the point that the presence of God can never be contained in or confined to one place. This is not because God's body is so large that it covers both Gerizim and Jerusalem at the same time but because *God is a spirit*.

Does this mean Jesus was implying that since God is a spirit and is to be worshiped in spirit and truth that there is no need for church buildings? No, there is nothing wrong with human beings having a special location for meeting together to worship God. God's being didn't change between the Old and New Testaments.

In Old Testament times the Spirit-God was worshiped in a physical place—not because He could be contained in a specific locality but because human beings are space-bound creatures. And the New Testament community of believers also continued the practice of meeting in assembly. They came to a certain *place* for worship. Jesus was not abolishing the use of places of worship but was correcting error that can slip into our thinking. We can easily think that by going to a certain place at a certain time to worship the living God, God's presence is limited to that place. Not so. His presence is not limited to any single place precisely because He is a spirit.

God As Spirit

Understanding the word *spirit* can be difficult because even in the Bible the word has more than one meaning. In ancient days the word for spirit was also used for the words *breath* and *wind*. When Jesus spoke to Nicodemus about being born of the Spirit, He said: "The wind blows where it wishes, and you hear the sound of it, but cannot tell where it comes from and where it goes. So is everyone who is born of the Spirit" (John 3:8).

The work of the Spirit *(pneuma)* is like the working of the wind *(pneuma)*. Elsewhere Jesus "breathed" on the disciples and said to them, "Receive the Holy Spirit" (John 20:22). This link between spirit, breath, and wind is found not only in the

Greek language but is present in the Hebrew tongue as well. As far back as the creation narrative, where God "breathed" the breath of life into man and man became a living spirit, we find this link.

But is this all the Bible means by 'spirit'? Is spirit some ghostlike substance, a gaseous form of matter? If so, spirit would merely be one type or form of matter. What is the matter with God's being a kind of gaseous matter? The matter with this is that gas is still matter. If gas is matter, then God could be confined to finite space; He would be a composite; He would have parts that fit together to make a whole; He could not be fully present at all times in all places.

More important to our understanding of God as spirit are the positive implications of His being a spirit. God's spirituality is the basis of His being personal. We rejoice that God is not some impersonal force, some nebulous "higher power" like energy. God is a person with whom we can have a personal relationship. His personal character is tied with His being a spirit.

We are, as we have already seen from Scripture, also spiritual beings. But we are finite spirits, contained within the limits of our bodies. If I were to ask you at this very minute "Where do you live?" what would you say?

Recently, at a meeting in Florida, I asked a woman that question and she replied, "I live in Philadelphia."

"Are you now in Philadelphia?" I responded.

She quickly replied, "No, I am in Orlando." (Her tone indicated that she was a bit annoyed by having to provide such an obvious answer.)

My next question was even more annoying: "Are you now alive?"

"Of course!" she said.

"Well if you live in Philadelphia, and you are not now in Philadelphia, how can you still be alive? You didn't bring Philadelphia with you to Orlando did you?" I concluded.

We both laughed at the nonsense I had made out of perfectly normal patterns of speech. When others ask where we live, we assume they want to know the location of our home. Our usual answer is quite valid. If we get technical, however, we must admit that we live wherever we are. We live within the confines of our bodies. Wherever our bodies go, we go.

So far there is no convincing evidence for astral projection. If I want to go to San Francisco, I can't send my spirit while my body stays home. My spirit indeed is capable of leaving my body. However, we don't call that astral projection; we call it death.

My life is contained within my body. I look forward to a time when my soul will temporarily be disunited from my body after it dies, and I am present in heaven. But even then I will look still further to the ultimate redemption of my body.

I live where I am. My consciousness is where life is made intelligible to me. My feelings may flow from my body, from my stomach, or from my leg, but my consciousness of these feelings is found in my mind. But what is my mind? It is certainly related to my brain, but can it be identified with my brain?

One of the most elusive of all philosophical matters is the nature of human personality and/or consciousness. Is there really such a thing as a self? The self cannot be studied and dissected like the heart or any other organ. But even though we cannot comprehend the full nature of the self or of human consciousness, just *consciously* asking questions about human consciousness demonstrates its existence. I am conscious of my consciousness. I can go no further.

To be sure skeptics have always denied the reality of a spiritual aspect to humanity. Crass materialists have always insisted that the sum of human life is matter—all life is physical, including appetites, feelings, and thoughts. Thought itself is described as merely a physical impulse without any significance or freedom. "We think what we think as a result of pure physical impulses and causes," this reasoning says.

One philosopher argued this viewpoint, but I've often wondered why he ever bothered to write a book about it. If all thoughts are the fixed results of physical causes, then the same would apply to the arguments of the philosopher who is making this claim. If all arguments flow out of physical causes, then there is no such thing as intelligible thinking; indeed, there is no such reality as thought itself. If thinking were merely mechanical, physical impulses and nothing more, then it would be foolish to even speak about sound thinking or false thinking.

Are we persuaded that thought is real? Yes, it is mysterious, but nevertheless it is real. In our thoughts, our consciousness, we experience the depth dimension of our own lives. Thought is connected to the brain, but it is not the brain. Consciousness and brain tissue are not the same thing.

Descartes was getting at this in his famous statement, "I think, therefore, I am." To be conscious of thought is to be conscious of our own existence. I know that I exist as a personal self because I am conscious of myself. Just doubting my consciousness of my self affirms my consciousness of my self. Without the capacity to think I cannot know myself. By thinking, I am immediately in touch with myself.

The Bible teaches that man is a physical, personal spirit. Our normal condition is for our spirits to dwell in our bodies. We "live" in our bodies. God is a nonphysical, personal spirit. The qualities of matter do not apply to Him. That God is spirit means that He does not have a body. He is immaterial.

Understanding the Reality We Cannot See

What is a nonphysical spirit? Here again is a very elusive concept—difficult for us because we are accustomed to thinking in physical terms. The physical is our reference point because we are physical creatures. Philosophers have sought to get at this idea in various ways. One is to distinguish between 'extension' and 'nonextension.' Matter is defined as that which has extension—it has size. A line that is extended can be measured. We can say that the line is ten miles long, ten feet long, or ten inches long.

That which is nonextended has no length. It cannot be measured. It takes up no space. It has no weight. It has none of the quantitative attributes of a physical or extended object.

Some might argue that if something has no extension it is simply nothing: 'Without extension' would mean 'without being.' No, 'without extension' simply means 'without physical being.' There is no reason to suppose that nonextended or spiritual being is impossible. This is at the very heart of the Christian faith. One of the Christian's boldest assertions is that there is a reality that far exceeds the visible reality of the physical world. In fact, the possibility of a nonphysical reality is demonstrated by the fact that our own humanity is impossible to discuss apart from the assumption that a nonextended reality—thought—exists.

Even modern science finds it necessary to speak of ultimate reality in spiritual terms. This was brought home to me vividly in a conversation I once had with a professor of physics. The professor was complaining that theology was not really a science because too many of its most basic concepts are far too vague to be scientific. He was specifically concerned about the very word *God*. He said, "The concept of God is so nebulous that it can mean almost anything. You theologians always seem to seek comfort in your assertion that God is a spirit. What is a spirit anyway?"

"You should be sympathetic with us," I replied. "You fellows in physics have the same problem. You are always talking about energy, and I have no idea what energy is."

"Oh, that's not the same problem. We know that energy is mc^2," he answered.

"Yes, I am aware of the mathematical formula, but I want to know what it is."

"The simple definition is that energy is the ability to do work," the man responded.

Again I persisted, "I don't want to know what it can do, I want to know what it is. What is its being? Its ontology? You fellows talk as if it were something. You call it a form of matter but it's not matter. Is it a spirit or what?"

The man grew silent. He began to feel the problem. All sciences use nonmaterial terms. Using the nonmaterial realm in our efforts to explain the material realm is inescapable.

Spirit Is Much More Than Force

Sometimes it is tempting to explain spirit by the concept of force. The Bible speaks of spiritual power, but speaking of spiritual power is not the same thing as saying "power power" or "spiritual spiritual." If spirit and power were identical we could not distinguish between them. It is one thing to say that a spirit can be powerful or that a spirit can generate power, but it is quite another to say that a spirit is power.

Power is mere force. Something must create or generate that power. The power itself is impersonal. The power flowing from human spirits is the power of thought, feeling, and will. We are aware of ourselves as persons when we think, feel, or act. Think of it! Have you ever been conscious of yourself in any other way?

When we say that God is a spirit we are saying more than that He is not physical and that He has power. We are saying that God is personal. If we are spiritual in our ability to think, feel, and act, how much more must God have these abilities? If He lacked the ability to think or be conscious of Himself, He would not be a spirit; He would be a mere force, unless His spirit were of a lower order than our own.

Because God is a personal spirit we can have a personal relationship with Him. He can communicate with us. It is not by accident that God is most concerned with what we think, what we feel, and what we choose (how we act). Our behavior concerns Him because our behavior is of a personal nature. Because God thinks and acts in personal relationships, we have a moral standard of behavior. Because God is a moral being, we are moral beings. Because God is holy, we are called to be holy.

If God were impersonal, it would not matter to Him how we behaved. He would not care because He *could not* care. He would be totally unconscious of who we were, let alone what we did or how we felt. Nothing could be worse than to discover that God is an impersonal spirit.

There is one category of human beings—unrepentant sinners who hope with all their might that God is not personal. If He is not personal, they need not fear that He might take their sin against Him personally. If God is impersonal who needs to fear the Last Judgment? Whatever you and I could get away with in this world we would have gotten away with now and forever. We would not need to fear a future bar of justice where we would be held accountable.

Part of the frightening teaching of Jesus is that every single, idle word flowing from our lips will be examined in the judgment by a personal, spiritual Creator. The one who is infinite Spirit will judge my spirit. He will judge my thoughts, my feelings, and my actions. He will judge them by the standard of His own thoughts and feelings and actions.

51

God's thoughts are pure; my thoughts are impure. God's actions are perfect; my actions are imperfect. That is why I need a Savior. That is why my spirit rejoices in God my Savior! A personal, spiritual God has provided a personal, spiritual redemption for me. Salvation involves the reconciliation of a relationship. To be saved means to be restored to fellowship with the living God. Fellowship is a personal relationship. I cannot be reconciled to an empty force; I cannot be estranged from a nameless power.

Because God is a spirit, I can have sweet communion with Him. I can think about His sweetness and have my emotions moved by His majesty. I can offer my choices, my willful decisions to Him. I can worship Him.

Worship is not only possible but necessary. God requires worship from us, but not any kind of worship will do. God is greatly concerned about the kind of worship we offer to Him. Jesus did not stop after declaring to the Samaritan woman that God is a spirit. He went on to say, "And those who worship Him must worship in spirit and truth" (John 4:24).

What God Wants in Worship

What does it mean to worship God in spirit and truth? Jesus did not say that we must worship God *as* spirit but *in* spirit. Our spirits are to offer praise to God as a spirit, not to come to Him through idolatry. Spiritual worship bars the use of idols.

Perhaps the oldest sin of man is idolatry. The tendency toward idolatry is not limited to primitive savages but is evident everywhere in the human bloodstream. The universal indictment Paul wrote to the human race in Romans 1 focuses on the sin of idolatry, which involves a violation of the first and second commandments.

The prohibition against using graven images or idols in worship was set forth most explicitly in the second commandment:

> You shall not make for yourself any carved image, or any likeness of anything that is in heaven above, or that is in the earth beneath, or that is in the water under the earth; you shall not bow down to them nor serve them. For I, the LORD your God,

am a jealous God, visiting the iniquity of the fathers on the children to the third and fourth generations of those who hate Me, but showing mercy to thousands, to those who love Me and keep My commandments.   *(Exod. 20:4–6)*

The Bible makes it clear that God commands everyone everywhere to worship Him. Worship is the duty of every creature. But any kind of worship is not enough. God commands us to worship Him in a proper manner. On the positive side, He commands worship in spirit and in truth. On the negative side, He prohibits the use of idols in worshiping Him. He knows we are prone to idolatry and that we are idol factories.

Idolatry in the Nation's Capitol

On a visit to Washington, D.C., once I took a guided tour of the Capitol. I was moved by the understated elegance of the furnishings of the original Senate chambers and the Supreme Court. I enjoyed the wealth of art works that adorn this history-packed building. The legends, the lore of the great oratory of Henry Clay, of Webster and Calhoun, all came alive.

My nostalgic and patriotic bubble burst, however, when we passed to the floor of the rotunda immediately beneath the vast dome that is the building's most recognizable feature. Our tour guide lifted her eyes toward the ceiling and pointed out the mural painted on the inside of the great Capitol dome. She told of the Herculean effort of the painter who created this masterpiece, rivaling the effort of Michelangelo in the Sistine Chapel. Then she announced the title of the painting: *The Apotheosis of George Washington*.

I was horror-stricken. Though I favor the separation of church and state, I was shocked to see the nation going this far in supporting a crass form of sheer idolatry. The principal meaning of *apotheosis* is "deification" or "elevation to divine status." I am aware that many Americans have never heard the term *apotheosis* and are not the least bit troubled by it. Surely our tour guide had no problems with it.

The mural displays George Washington being welcomed into the pantheon of gods by other pagan deities. History indicates that although George Washington was a member in good standing of the Episcopal church, he was no great zealot in religious matters. Nevertheless, I cannot imagine our first president being anything but mortified by such a work of art. To suggest to George Washington that he might be worthy of deification would be to insult him profoundly. Such a work also is an insult to the moral sensibilities and the intelligence of the American people. And we may be assured that it is an insult to God. That this offensive painting is viewed daily by multitudes of Christians without any murmur or complaint underlines in red the prevailing cavalier attitude regarding idolatry.

It is no wonder God declares Himself a jealous God. He is jealous for the integrity of His own Being. Obviously we are not so inclined to jealousy in His behalf. Michelangelo's masterpiece in the Sistine Chapel ceiling depicts the act of God's creation of Adam. Here the Deity is painted in human form, a clear and violent prohibition of the second commandment. We are not to use images of God in worship. God is to be worshiped in spirit and truth.

Idolatry is a form of worship, but it is false worship that distorts the character of God and violates God's majesty. It involves what the Apostle Paul called "exchanging the truth for the lie" (Rom. 1:25).

> Although they knew God, they did not glorify Him as God, nor were thankful, but became futile in their thoughts, and their foolish hearts were darkened. Professing to be wise, they became fools, and changed the glory of the incorruptible God into an image made like corruptible man—and birds and four-footed beasts and creeping things. Therefore God also gave them up to uncleanness, in the lusts of their hearts, to dishonor their bodies among themselves, who exchanged the truth of God for the lie, and worshiped and served the creature rather than the Creator, who is blessed forever. Amen.
>
> *(Rom. 1:21–25)*

God is not pleased with some forms of worship. False worship is a dreadful insult to Him. Worship that is neither spiritual nor true is not acceptable. Indications that some acts of "worship" are unacceptable to God appear early in the Bible: "Abel also brought of the firstlings of his flock and of their fat. *And the* LORD *respected Abel and his offering*, but *He did not respect* Cain and his offering. And Cain was very angry, and his countenance fell" (Gen. 4:4–5, italics mine).

In this biblical episode Cain responded with anger. Presumably, he was filled with anger and jealousy toward his brother, Abel, whom he later savagely murdered. It is likely, though, he also was angry with God. Human beings tend to think that God is obligated to receive worship whether or not it is true and acceptable.

An ongoing issue regarding worship in our nation is prayer in the public schools. Decades ago when prayer was allowed in the public schools, classes began daily with "opening exercises." These usually included a reading from the Bible, a prayer, and the Pledge of Allegiance. When prayer and Bible reading were subsequently ruled out of order, many Christians were very upset. Today many evangelical Christians are agitating to restore the practice of prayer and Bible reading to public schools. Some wish only to make it permissible for Christians to pray and to hold their own Bible studies. Others want the full restoration of the traditional procedure. Anyone wanting to mandate prayer should answer these questions. Do we, as Christians, believe that God requires all men to worship Him in spirit and in truth? The answer, obviously, is yes. Do we not also agree that God does not accept false worship? I trust we agree on that point. My main question then is this: If God does not accept false worship, indeed is provoked by it, why would we urge people who are not Christians to pray?

To be sure, we are to urge non-Christians to become Christians and then to pray as Christians. But we must not urge them to pray as non-Christians. When we do this we are urging our fellow non-Christian human beings to invite the wrath of God upon themselves. Unless we believe that God is honored by worship that is other than what He prescribes, we ought not to force non-Christians to engage in false worship.

I am certain that the Christians who urge prayer in the public schools are doing so for noble reasons. Some merely are asking that the rights of Christians be restored and the growing persecution of Christianity in the secular school system be stopped. These are fighting with the angels. But others who crusade for the full restoration of imposed prayer are doing so, sadly, with little regard for God's requirements for acceptable worship. God is a spirit. Our worship of Him must be in spirit and in truth.

Because God is spirit, He has no body. He cannot be divided into parts or components. We see that He is personal. He is conscious and active even as we are. We see that it is possible for us to have a personal relationship with God. We see also that at the heart of the personal relationship is the practice of worship. We see that God requires not only that men worship Him but that we worship Him in a way that is acceptable to Him. God absolutely forbids the use of idols in worship. Our worship is to be spiritual as He is spiritual. Our worship is to be in truth as He is truth. To worship God in truth is to worship Him in the way that He commands. To worship Him in any other way is to be involved in false worship, worship against the truth.

The Holy Spirit

The Scriptures have much to say concerning the Person and work of the Holy Spirit. The teachings regarding the Spirit are so important that they deserve a separate volume. We touch only lightly now on the Holy Spirit insofar as He is related to the divine attribute of spirit.

If one member of the Trinity is called the Spirit or the Holy Spirit, may we conclude that the other two members are not spirit? No. All three members of the Trinity are God. The Father is God; the Son is God; and the Spirit is God. What is true of God is true of all members of the Godhead. God is a spirit. That means that the Father is spirit, the Son (touching His divine nature) is spirit, and the Spirit is spirit.

The Holy Spirit is both spirit and holy, as His name indicates. But the Father and the Son are also holy. Though it is necessary to make personal distinctions in the Godhead, we must remember that these distinctions of personality do not fragment the essence of God. The Father is spirit; the Son is spirit; the Spirit is spirit. This is not to say, however, that the Father is the Son and the Father is the Holy Spirit. If we did

Not unto us, O Lord, not unto us,
But to Your name give glory,
Because of Your mercy,
And because of Your truth.
Why should the Gentiles say,
"Where now is their God?"
But our God is in heaven;
He does whatever He pleases.
Their idols are silver and gold,
The work of men's hands.
They have mouths, but they do not speak;
Eyes they have, but they do not see;
They have ears, but they do not hear;
Noses they have, but they do not smell;
They have hands, but they do not handle;
Feet they have, but they do not walk;
Nor do they mutter through their throat.
Those who make them are like them;
So is everyone who trusts in them.

. . . .

You who fear the Lord, trust in the Lord;
He is their help and their shield.

. . . .

May you be blessed by the Lord,
Who made heaven and earth.
The heaven, even the heavens, are the Lord's
But the earth He has given to the children of men.
The dead do not praise the Lord,
Nor any who go down into silence.
But we will bless the Lord
From this time forth and forevermore.
Praise the Lord!

Psalm 115:1–8, 11, 15–18

this, we would obscure the personal distinctions of the triune God.

We have seen that God is spirit. We have also noted that as human beings we are spiritual. We have a personal spirit within us. We are finite spirits. God is an infinite spirit. God's spirit is both infinite and eternal. He is also invisible. These characteristics of His spiritual nature require that we search further and dig deeper in our effort to know Him.

How Much Do You Know, God?

"I have nothing to hide; my life is an open book." How many times have you heard someone make that remark? How many times have you or I said that ourselves? We may say we have nothing to hide, but that does not make it so. Every life has a closet.

We are all fugitives, fleeing to our favorite hiding places. We hide from our spouses, from our parents, and from our friends. Although we may have one or two close confidants with whom we discuss some of our deep, dark secrets, none of us has a human friend to whom we tell everything. We can't even bear to tell everything to ourselves. Some of our impulses are too embarrassing to confess.

Are you like me—wanting people to know me by my virtues rather than my vices? I want to have a good reputation, not a bad one. Yet every person of good repute could lose that reputation instantly if the full truth were known. All of us are vulnerable to blackmail, and the truth is that we go to great pains to cover our less virtuous acts. We all have our own private Watergates.

When I was a child, a Sunday school teacher told me that the invisible God could see everything I did. Nothing was hidden from His eyes. That was not "great news." To make matters worse, I was told that God could even read my mind. It was as if God were a superhuman Dunninger, the ultimate Great Kreskin. He could think my private thoughts with me. God seemed to be a year-round Santa Claus, a three-hundred-and-sixty-five-day-a-year list maker. God had a book in which He recorded each of my sins with an indelible black mark. (In my mind His book was like those dreadful black books my elementary school teachers carried about.) God was making a list and checking it twice. That terrified me.

As I grew older my concept of God grew up as well. At some point I discarded the notion of a bearded man with a little black book and an indelible pen. I studied theology in college, seminary, and graduate school. My concept of God became more refined, more sophisticated, more cerebral. But I still was not able to escape the truth that, in fact, God does know everything about me. And I discovered that He didn't need a black book to remember the data but, to my everlasting relief, I also discovered that His pen did not contain indelible ink.

David learned the same things about God. He sang of them in the Psalms:

"O LORD, You have searched me and known me.
You know my sitting down and my rising up;
You understand my thought afar off.
You comprehend my path and my lying down,
And are acquainted with all my ways.
For there is not a word on my tongue,
But behold, O LORD, You know it altogether.
You have hedged me behind and before,
And laid Your hand upon me.
Such knowledge is too wonderful for me;
It is high, I cannot attain it.   *(Ps. 139:1–6)*

What David sang about in poetry was declared in bold prose by Jesus when He warned that everything hidden will be revealed at the Last Judgment. Jesus declared that even every careless word uttered would be brought into account. Nothing escapes the eye of God. Our every thought, every act, every word will be examined on judgment day.

If there were no final, ultimate judgment day, then God's total knowledge of my life would not be so threatening. Or if He knew all things but were not all-powerful, I might be less intimidated. Or even if He were omniscient and omnipotent but not altogether holy, I might have a chance to negotiate a few things. However, He is all of these things and unchangeably so.

Will Christians Face Judgment?

Many Christians take comfort in the incorrect belief that Christians will not have to be present at the Last Judgment. Some people believe that this is what we are "saved" from. Not so. We are spared the wrath of God, and we are justified. That means we will escape divine condemnation, but we will still be held accountable before God. We must all face the divine scrutiny.

In our lifetime, few of us are ever exposed to a formal trial by jury, but we are judged in many ways. School teachers, employers or bosses, military superior officers, and other authority figures evaluate our performance. These judgments are not always accurate, and at times they reflect bias, ignorance, or prejudice. We can never depend upon their absolute fairness.

With God we face an absolutely just evaluation. There will be no bias, no prejudice, no unfairness. The color of our skin, how much money we have, how beautiful our face—nothing will affect God's complete fairness. In this judgment the evaluation will be more than accurate; it will be infallible.

The idea of an infallible judgment for every person was at the heart of Jesus' teaching. He warned of the ultimate crisis for mankind. The very word *crisis* comes from the Greek word *krisis* which means "judgment." Today, the Christian church rarely emphasizes the notion of a last judgment. The idea is not very popular. People do not want to think about being held accountable for their lives. Yet the concept of ultimate accountability was clearly taught by Jesus.

God's Omniscience

In my book *If There Is a God, Why Are There Atheists?* (Minneapolis: Bethany Fellowship, 1978), I discussed the thoughts of the French philosopher Jean Paul Sartre.

In Sartre's book *Being and Nothingness,* he included an interesting study of the omniscience of God. He likened God to a cosmic voyeur. God peers down from heaven and watches everything we do. Sartre saw this concept of God as radically dehumanizing and complained that beneath the gaze of such a God, man would be reduced to a mere object, to a thing that could be analyzed and scrutinized like frogs in a biology lab. It was as though God were peeping through a keyhole looking at us and stripping us naked under His omniscient gaze.

Sartre's treatment of God's omniscience brilliantly captured the frightening terror of guilt that plagues us. Sartre reconstructed that awful sense of shame that entered the experience of humanity in Eden.

In the Creation we were made naked and unashamed. The first sin brought with it the first human experience of shame, expressed in terms of an awareness of nakedness. Guilt was born. We have not escaped its power yet. We still long for a place where we can be naked and not ashamed. We still long to be in the garden with God where His presence does not chill us with terror.

To be known by God is an idea that divides the human race. There are those who long to be known by God. For we Christians there is no greater solace than to know we are known by God and still loved. For unbelievers nothing is more dreadful than the thought of being known completely by God. The pagan does not want God to look at him; he wants God to overlook him.

The Bible declares that the wicked flee when no one pursues (see Prov. 28:1). This reveals the power of guilt to unsettle us. The sinner must master the art of the backward glance in order to survive. Luther put it another way: "The pagan trembles at the rustling of a leaf."

What are we afraid of? We are afraid of the relentless pursuit of an omniscient God, a God who knows everything. I am embarrassed by my nakedness. There are many things in my life that I do not want to put under the gaze of Christ. Yet I know there is nothing hidden from Him. He knows me better than my wife knows me. And yet He loves me. This is the most amazing thing of all about God's grace. It would be one thing for Him to love us if we could fool Him into thinking that we were better than we actually are. But He knows better. He knows all there is to know about us, including those things that could destroy our reputation. He is minutely and acutely aware of every skeleton in every closet. And He loves us.

Once we understand that God is for us then our natural fear of His gaze is lessened. We can even say with David,

Search me, O God, and know my heart;
Try me and know my anxieties.
And see if there is any wicked way in me,
And lead me in the way everlasting.

(Ps. 139:23–24)

Do you see the stark contrast between the attitude of David and someone like Jean Paul Sartre? David asked God to shine His searchlight on his soul. David willingly submitted to the gaze of God and desired the divine scrutiny. He even asked to be put on trial. David did not do this arrogantly, daring God to find anything wrong. On the contrary, David knew that God would find wicked ways in his heart, and he wanted to be made clean. David wanted to be purified not only from conscious sins but from secret faults as well. He welcomed the gaze of God because he had experienced it before and knew that it brought healing.

To be known by God is our highest privilege. The deepest folly of man is to flee from the eye of God. Hiding from God is as foolish as it is futile. There is no adequate hiding place. We can call for the mountains to fall upon us and the hills to cover us. But the eye of God can see through mountains and penetrate the cloak of hills.

There is only one adequate cloak for our shame—the righteousness of Christ. Our nakedness and shame are covered by a shield that no guilt can pierce. Our lives are hid in Him. He is our refuge. He who knows the fugitive's crime gives the fugitive a hiding place.

Science and Omniscience

The conflict between science and religion is a strange thing. The battles have been numerous and fierce, causing some to divorce science from faith. When this occurs, science becomes the province of reason, and religion becomes the arena of blind faith. What a tragic state of affairs this is for those whose faith is confident of divine omniscience.

God is a God of knowledge. He is concerned with science, indeed, He invented science. The root word of *science* means simply "to know." Science is the business of acquiring knowledge. That knowledge may be in biology, astronomy, economics, or mathematics. If God is truth, then all true knowledge tells us something about God Himself. As the fathers declared, "All truth meets at the top." All truth is ultimately God's truth.

This means that ultimately there can be no conflict between genuine science and the truth of God. Christians may have something to fear from certain scientists, but they have nothing to fear from authentic science. Christians should be the avant-garde of science. Of all people, they should be the most zealously dedicated to the pursuit of truth.

The conflict we Christians have with science at times is linked to the fact that not one of us is omniscient. We gain knowledge but we do not have all knowledge. Each of us is capable of being corrected.

What happens when theologians and scientists disagree? If the disagreement involves a contradiction, then we know one thing for sure: Somebody is wrong. Both the scientist and the theologian are creatures with limited knowledge. Neither of them is omniscient. If theology and science are to have fruitful discussion, there is need for humility on both sides.

There have been times in church history when theologians got egg on their faces for disputing with scientists; the theologians should have been doing less arguing and more listening. There are also times when scientists need to listen to theologians.

What if scientists teach something that is contrary to the Bible? There is an easy answer and a more difficult answer. First, the easy answer. If the Bible is the Word of God and if God is omniscient, then the obvious answer is: The scientist who teaches contrary to the Bible is wrong. It takes little intellectual acumen to realize that a fallible person can never correct an infallible person. So it is likewise impossible that an omniscient deity could ever be corrected by men who are not omniscient.

Again, I am not suggesting that theologians are infallible and scientists are fallible or that it is impossible for a scientist to correct a theologian. No, God alone is omniscient. Scientists may correct theologians, but they may never correct God.

If the Bible is the Word of God (which I certainly believe), then no scientist or group of scientists may ever correct it. If the Bible is God's truth no scientific discovery can ever refute or contradict it. Truth is coherent. Truth is consistent with other truth. If truth is ever contradictory, then truth itself is manifestly impossible. Here we meet an all or nothing situation, a true dilemma. If one real contradiction exists within the sum of truth, then we can never know any truth, for whatever truth we think we know may have a contradictory that is also true.

That was the easy answer to our question, What if scientists teach something that is contrary to the Bible? The hard answer rests in the complexities found in our understanding of the Bible and our understanding of science. Theologians can and do make mistakes in interpreting the Bible. Those mistaken interpretations can be corrected with the knowledge made available to us from science. By the same token, we know that scientists also make mistakes. Although science is often presented as a guileless, unhindered quest for knowledge, the history of science abounds with rigid orthodoxy, prejudicial dogmatism, and narrow-minded bigotry. Pet theories die hard in the natural sciences. And scientists also are capable of misinterpreting the data.

I say confidently that all truth is coherent because I know that all truth flows ultimately from God. God Himself is coherent and consistent. There is no confusion in Him. God views everything from the vantage point of eternity. There are no limits to His vision, no blindspots in His viewpoint.

God's knowledge of the natural order is the knowledge of the Creator. He knows the intricacies of the universe the way a cabinetmaker knows the grooves of the woods he shapes. Every detail of chemistry is known perfectly by God. What fills the largest libraries or most gigantic computers is known exhaustively by God.

The practical implications of God's omniscience are overwhelming. We seek advice from people in this world who have demonstrated that they have a high degree of knowledge and wisdom. Corporations pay huge sums of money to hire consultants who are acknowledged experts in their fields. Knowledge is worth money; it is a valuable commodity. We make life and death decisions because of confidence in other people's knowledge.

But all human knowledge is limited—limited by perspective and limited in strength. No man's perspective is eternal or infinite. Our viewpoint is always finite and short-range. We each contribute some proof to the maxim *errare humanum est*— "to err is human." We do not say that "to err is divine." To assign error to God is to insult His majesty.

Forever, O Lord,
Your word is settled in heaven.
Your faithfulness endures to all generations;
You established the earth, and it abides.
They continue this day according to Your ordinances,
For all are Your servants.
Unless Your law had been my delight,
I would then have perished in my affliction.
I will never forget Your precepts,
For by them You have given me life.
I am Yours, save me;
For I have sought Your precepts.
The wicked wait for me to destroy me,
But I will consider Your testimonies.
I have seen the consummation of all perfection,
But Your commandment is exceedingly broad.

Psalm 119:89–96

Where Is Truth, God?

One of the more heated controversies of our day involves the Bible. Is the Bible inspired? Is the Bible infallible? Is the Bible inerrant? These questions hinge upon a more basic question: Is the Bible the Word of God?

We all know that the Bible was written by human beings. The human authors wrote human words with human pens. None of the human authors was omniscient. Yet these human writings claim to be more than mere human opinions. Jeremiah did not preface his prophetic utterances by saying, "In my opinion," or "It is my considered judgment that." He prefaces his declarations by saying, "Thus saith the Lord."

The Bible's claim to speak with more authority than the authority of human insight or opinion was stated succinctly by the Apostle Paul: "All Scripture is given by inspiration of God, and is profitable for doctrine, for reproof, for correction, for instruction in righteousness, that the man of God may be complete, thoroughly equipped for every good work" (2 Tim. 3:16–17).

Here the Bible claims that Scripture is given by *inspiration*. The word here literally means "God-breathed." *To inspire* something means "to breathe" into it. The word Paul used, however, is not the word for breathing *in* but for breathing *out*. A more literal translation would be "all Scripture is given by *expiration*."

What difference does it make whether we speak of inspiration or expiration? A significant difference. Our doctrine of inspiration involves God's aiding human authors by supervising their work; the Holy Spirit worked upon and in the human writers to insure that what they wrote was the Word of God.

On the other hand, the term *expiration* does not refer to God's activity in the work of the human writers but rather to the source of Scripture. When Paul said that all Scripture is "God-breathed," he was saying that the source of all Scripture is God.

In our own experience, when people dispute the accuracy of a report or a claim, they want to know the source of the information. In college our term papers had to have a fitting number of footnotes to document the information sources. The quest for source is a quest for the basis of the claim. Is the claim based upon hearsay? Is the claim based upon the ravings of a lunatic? Is the claim based upon a credible expert in the field?

We seek the source of claims to truth because we want to know if the claims are credible. The newspaper writer loves an "unimpeachable source." Somehow an unimpeachable source is much more comforting than an "unnamed source." But even an unnamed source is better than an "unreliable source."

Before I commit my life to some claim, I want to be sure that the claim is not being made by an unreliable source. What the Apostle Paul is saying to Timothy is that the source of the Bible is God. The source of the Bible is not merely unimpeachable and reliable; the source is omniscient. It is precisely because the source is omniscient that we expect the Bible to be unimpeachable and reliable. If the source of the Bible were human, we would be foolish to argue for its infallibility.

Many scholars within the church no longer believe that the Bible is infallible or inerrant. They have come to the conclusion that Paul was wrong. They are not at all persuaded that the Scriptures are inspired. These scholars are consistent in their criticism. They say that the Bible was never inspired and that, therefore, there is no reason to assume that it reflects anything more than human insight and opinion. Since human opinion can and often does err, there is no reason to argue for the inerrancy of these opinions.

There is another group, however, who holds a most strange, indeed bizarre, view of the Bible. This group believes that the Bible is inspired of God but still errs. On the one hand they speak fervently about the wonderful message of the Word of God, while on the other hand they complain about its faulty elements.

I once heard a church historian explain this view by writing the following formula on the blackboard: THE WORD OF GOD, WHICH ERRS. The historian then went to the blackboard with an eraser and erased "The word of," the comma, and the "which," leaving just two words, "God Errs." He explained that such an assertion was simply unacceptable to the Christian and articulated a monstrous insult to God. The professor insisted that if the Bible is the Word of God, then the Bible does not err. If the Bible errs then it is not the Word of God. An errant Bible may give us an insightful message or word *about* God, but it cannot be the word *of* God.

Some Christians have become so confused about this that they say the Bible is infallible but it is not inerrant. Imagine, if you can (be alarmed if you can), an infallible Bible that errs. An infallible Bible that errs is like an immovable object that rolls away. The term *infallible* is a stronger term than the term *inerrant*. To say that something is inerrant is simply to say that it does not err. To say that something is infallible is to say that it cannot err. Obviously, if something cannot err, one can never say that it errs.

Those who claim that the Bible is infallible but not inerrant will immediately cry foul because I have just made their position appear silly. They will defend themselves by arguing that they do not mean by the word *infallible* that the Bible cannot err. Never mind that the word *infallible* in all of history has always meant precisely that. Never mind that people understand the word *infallible* to mean that it cannot err. They want the word to have a different meaning.

If this is their reply, I will retract my criticism that their view is silly. If they mean by infallible something other than that the Bible cannot err, then their view is not silly: It is dishonest. This is an outright deception that should not be perpetrated by honorable people.

73

The meaning of three closely related concepts must be kept clear in our minds. These concepts include the words 1) *omniscient,* 2) *infallible,* and 3) *inerrant.* To be omniscient means that one knows everything. On the surface it appears that if someone were omniscient he also would have to be infallible and inerrant. But what if the omniscient one were evil? There would be no guarantee that his pronouncements were true.

I do not believe for a second that an omniscient being who is evil exists. Yes, the devil exists; the devil is evil. But the devil is not omniscient. He is a creature. He is finite. His knowledge may be greater than ours, but his knowledge is limited.

Only God is omniscient. God is also righteous. He is altogether righteous. If, therefore, God is both righteous and omniscient, we can expect that any information coming from Him is most certainly infallible and inerrant.

We have already seen that infallible describes an *ability.* Someone who is infallible has the ability *never* to fail. He cannot err. It is possible to be inerrant without being infallible, but it is not possible to be infallible without also being inerrant. I can be inerrant within limits. I have made 100 percent on spelling tests. I have written inerrant grocery lists. But neither of these less than prodigious feats qualifies me for the grand term of infallibility.

God is omniscient; He knows everything. God is infallible; it is impossible for Him to fail. God is inerrant; He never errs. Not only does God not commit error, but He does not inspire error. God is neither the source of nor the inspirer of error. What comes from His divine mind is truth. What He inspires is truth. The professor was right: If a book has errors, it is not the Word of God. If a book is the Word of God, it does not have errors. We cannot have a book that is both the Word of God and errant. Surely, it is possible to conceive of *a book* that is partly errant and partly the Word of God. But I do not think the Bible is that sort of a book. The only point I am pleading for is that we be clear in understanding that whatever is inspired is not errant. God does not commit errors or induce human authors to commit errors.

God Knows What He Is Talking About

Why is God's omniscience so extremely relevant to our understanding of the Bible? We are often asked to stand on the teaching of the Bible or to stand on the opinions of experts who disagree with the Bible.

Is premarital sex healthy or not? I have read the judgments of psychiatrists who claim that under certain conditions premarital sex is not only permissible but a positive contribution to a healthy marriage.

On the other hand, the New Testament takes a different view. The Apostle Paul wrote, "But fornication and all uncleanness or covetousness, let it not even be named among you, as is fitting for saints" (Eph. 5:3).

Now we have conflict. Leading experts tell us that fornication is all right. They are joined by a chorus of educators and even some clergy. We add to this the reports of sexual historians, like Kinsey and Chapman, who have surveyed modern Americans and discovered that the vast majority have practiced premarital sex. This is true outside the church and inside the church as well.

The statistical information seems so overwhelming—is the Bible giving bad advice here? Is this just Paul's opinion, or is it the Word of God? If it is the Word of God, why is it so out of sync with modern theory and practice?

One answer we cannot give is that the Bible is wrong because God doesn't understand human nature. Remember, if God is omniscient, He knows what He is talking about.

God knows what He is talking about. That is the heart of the practical implications of God's omniscience. We can absolutely trust His advice. He knows more than the educators, more than the American Psychiatric Association, more than a symposium of learned clergymen, more than newspaper columnists or TV talk show hosts. If every scholar in the world agreed that premarital sex was good and God said it was bad, would there be any contest?

As a pastor I have encountered conflict between what Scripture enjoins and what human opinion suggests. These conflicts are often in serious matters that cannot be treated lightly. I have found my own instincts in counseling clearly in conflict with what I knew the Scriptures to teach. It is at this point that we run head-on into our view of the Scripture and our view of God. Humility demands that we bow before the One who is omniscient.

All of God's laws reflect His perfect omniscience. But His law also reflects His benevolence, His love for us. God's law is not only brilliant but kind. God, being omniscient, not only *knows* what is best for me but, in His kindness, *wants* what is best for me. This is a difficult idea to swallow because it is virtually built into our fallen natures to think that God's law is against us. *If God really loved us, His law would not be so restrictive*, we tend to think. But He prohibits sin not because sin enhances human life but because it destroys human life. God knows that. God knows what He is doing.

God's Riches of Wisdom and Knowledge

In human terms there is a great divide between knowledge and wisdom. We know people who are quite knowledgeable but who lack common sense. Brilliant people often act in foolish ways. A person can have great knowledge and lack wisdom. We cannot have wisdom without knowledge, but we can have knowledge without wisdom.

In God there is no divorce of wisdom and knowledge. God is both all-knowing and all-wise. His consummate wisdom is in perfect harmony with His consummate knowledge. We cannot be His guidance counselors.

The word *philosophy* means literally "the love of wisdom." True biblical wisdom is found in the love and reverence of God. Hebrew wisdom sees a foundational principle in the fear of God. "The fear of the LORD is the beginning of wisdom" (Ps. 111:10). To have no fear of God is not wise. People who do not believe in God are not necessarily stupid. Some very knowledgeable and very bright people do not affirm the existence of God. No, they are not stupid; they are foolish.

In biblical categories, foolishness is a sin. The fool's problem is not with his brain but with his heart. His mind is capable of grasping the things of God, but he has no desire for the things of God. The fool has no fear of or reverence for God.

For the Christian God's knowledge and wisdom provoke great joy. We delight in our "God only wise." We stand in awe before His transcendent wisdom. We join in the apostolic song of amazement: "Oh, the depth of the riches both of the wisdom and knowledge of God!" (Rom. 11:33).

How Much Did Jesus Know?

Was Jesus omniscient? Did the Baby in the manger know that the world was round?

The answer we give to these questions reveals much about our understanding of Christ. For centuries Christians have confessed their faith in Jesus by affirming that He is both human and divine. He is the God-man. We know that omniscience is a divine attribute. But did Jesus know everything?

We must carefully answer this question. Obviously from the New Testament portrait of Jesus, He displayed a remarkable knowledge of some things. He knew all about the Samaritan woman's sordid life. He knew the character of Nathaniel before He ever met him. On numerous occasions Jesus displayed supernatural knowledge. However, on one occasion He gave a surprising answer to a question: " 'But of that day and hour no one knows, neither the angels in heaven, nor the Son, but only the Father' " (Mark 13:32).

The disciples had asked Jesus some questions about His future return. He gave them some information but stopped short of naming the day and the hour. This information, He declared, was known only by the Father. Jesus indicated a limit to His own knowledge.

How are we to understand this? If Jesus was God incarnate, should not all of God's divine attributes have been present in Him? The great Roman Catholic scholar Saint Thomas Aquinas was deeply troubled by this question. Thomas took the position that Jesus really did know the day and the hour. He had to know because of the perfect unity that existed between His divine nature and human nature. Thomas explained that this knowledge was so high, so holy, so beyond the grasp of mortal men that there was no way that Jesus could communicate it. Therefore, He accommodated Himself to their human weakness by saying that He didn't know the day or the hour.

This is an unacceptable explanation for obvious reasons. No matter what you call this "act of accommodation," if this were His motive Jesus simply lied. He told the disciples that He didn't know something that in fact He did know. For whatever reason, if the incarnation of truth here violates the truth, then Jesus disqualifies Himself as our Savior.

There has to be a better explanation. Protestant scholars have taken a different position from that of the Roman Catholic church. Their answer has been that Jesus really didn't know the day and the hour—that is, touching His human nature, Jesus was not omniscient. Obviously Jesus' divine nature would have been omniscient. Omniscience is an attribute of God. But His human nature existed under the limitations of human nature. In His humanity Jesus was not omniscient.

How does this reasoning affect the unity of the two natures of Christ? Are we guilty of breaking that unity, of divorcing the divine and human natures? Not at all. We are not dividing the two natures; we are distinguishing between them.

In searching for an understanding of Jesus, we must be willing to make certain distinctions. For example, when Jesus grew weary, or hungry, we must understand that those experiences were evidence of His human nature. We know that God does not get hungry or sleepy. The tears of Jesus, the sweat of Jesus, the hunger of Jesus were all manifestations of His human nature. They were manifestations of a human nature that was in perfect unity with a divine nature. But His sweat was not divine sweat nor His tears divine tears.

The church struggled deeply with questions like these in the fifth century. The great Council of Chalcedon in 451 set forth some vitally important affirmations about the mystery of the Incarnation. Chalcedon declared that Jesus was *vere homo, vere deus*. That is, Jesus is "truly man and truly God."

Chalcedon also set up boundaries for our reflection about Jesus by establishing four watchdogs. These watchdogs are the "Four Negatives" of Chalcedon—the things we dare not do when discussing the human and divine natures of Jesus— 1) mixture, 2) confusion, 3) separation, and 4) division.

If we are to think properly about Jesus, we must never confuse the two natures or mix them together. To confuse them or to mix them up would be to violate both the deity and humanity of Christ. It would involve us in deifying His human nature or humanizing His divine nature. If we do either, we are left with a Christ who is not divine or human but some sort of bizarre hybrid.

On the other hand, if we separate or divide the two natures of Jesus, we fracture the unity of His person. Chalcedon put up this warning signal to protect against the idea that in Jesus the divine nature and the human nature were two different persons. The church believes that in Jesus we meet One who is both divine and human. Jesus has two natures but only one Person, and separating or dividing the two destroys the personal unity of Christ.

Again we must think carefully here. It is one thing to distinguish the two natures and quite another to separate or divide them. We can distinguish our bodies and our souls without harming anybody. But if we separate our bodies from our souls, we die.

Chalcedon concluded by adding another very important declaration: "Each nature retained its own attributes." This means that the divine nature did not stop being divine in the Incarnation and that the human nature did not suddenly become divine.

We see, then, that attributing omniscience to the human nature of Jesus would be deifying the human nature and confusing or mixing the divine nature. Saint Thomas thought that if we did not attribute omniscience to Jesus we would be guilty of dividing the two natures. The best thing to do in this case is to let Jesus tell us about the matter.

How Jesus Views the Bible

The issue of Jesus' omniscience is at the heart of the controversy over the Bible. We have already seen that if the Bible is the Word of God, then the Bible cannot err. But why did the Church ever start believing that the Bible was the Word of God in the first place? The simplest answer is that Jesus taught that the Bible was the Word of God.

Someone might ask, "How do we know what Jesus said about the Bible except by reading the Bible? Are we not involved here in a vicious sort of circular reasoning?"

The reasoning process here is not circular but linear. We begin with a basic study of the text of Scripture. First we ask, "Is the Bible a basically reliable historical document?" We are not asking if the Bible is the Word of God or infallible, only if it is basically trustworthy. If it's not we will have nothing more to do with it or with the Jesus it proclaims.

If it is basically reliable, then we can discuss what we know about Jesus of Nazareth. If, on the basis of reliable historical information, we conclude that Jesus taught that our source was not only reliable as a human document but absolutely reliable as the Word of God, then we have progressed in linear fashion. Ours is not circular reasoning.

The omniscience of Jesus fits into the debate about the Bible at a crucial point. Many, if not all, critics of the view that the Bible is the inerrant Word of God admit that Jesus taught a high view of Scripture. Jesus shared His contemporary Jewish community's high view of the Bible. Jesus said that the Scripture could not be broken. He referred to it as "Thy Word," indicating God. He spoke of every jot and tittle of the law being fulfilled. He hinged His debates with Satan and with the Pharisees on the turn of a single Old Testament word. We know that Jesus regarded the Bible as the Word of God and that He taught His disciples that view.

Was Jesus wrong in His view of the Bible? A host of prominent biblical scholars and theologians answer with a resounding yes. They do not shrink from saying He was wrong because they believe Jesus had limits to His knowledge. They argue that Jesus did not know the world was round. He had no way of knowing that Moses was not really the author of the first five books of the Old Testament. Jesus, in His human nature, was subject to all the errors of His contemporaries. His accepting and adopting the Jewish view of the Bible was to be expected since He was a human being who was not omniscient.

The point of the critics is clear: Jesus was wrong in His view of Scripture, but it's all right that He was wrong. Jesus has the scholars' permission to be wrong. He is excused on the grounds that He was not omniscient.

The critics are correct in saying that the human Jesus was not omniscient. I doubt if the human Jesus knew that the earth was round. But the issue is not that simple. We cannot dismiss the teaching of Jesus about the Bible because Jesus was not omniscient. Not only must we grapple with Jesus' omniscience, but we must also ask about His infallibility.

The Infallible Christ

What is often overlooked in the discussion about Jesus' view of the Bible is the moral issue of His teaching. The question is this: If Jesus taught things that were not true, are there any moral implications to this? The critics say no, excusing Jesus' errors on the basis of His lack of omniscience. Will such an excuse help me on judgment day? The Bible teaches that not many should become teachers because with teaching comes a greater responsibility. God does not expect me to be an omniscient teacher. He does not expect me to be an infallible teacher. But God does expect me to be a responsible teacher.

A responsible teacher is careful not to claim more knowledge than he actually has. A responsible teacher doesn't bluff his way with students, masking his ignorance. The question we face with Jesus is not, Was Jesus omniscient? but Was Jesus a responsible teacher?

Jesus made astonishing claims about His teaching. He claimed that He spoke nothing on His own authority but rather on the authority of God (see John 12:49). Here Jesus did not claim omniscience, but He did claim infallibility. To speak nothing except what is spoken on divine authority is surely to speak with utter infallibility. Jesus boldly proclaimed to be the Truth incarnate. He didn't merely declare that He spoke truth or that He knew truth; He asserted that He was the Truth.

Let us consider this for a moment. Suppose a man told you that every word he spoke had divine authority. Suppose he said to you that he was the incarnate Truth. Then suppose he told you all sorts of things about the Bible that, in fact, were not true. What would you think of this man as a teacher? Would you say as Nicodemus said of Jesus, "Rabbi, we know that You are a teacher come from God" (John 3:2)?

The issue here is not so much the reliability of Jesus as the Supreme Teacher of the church. The real issue is the reliability of Jesus as Savior. If Jesus claimed to have more knowledge than He actually had, if He claimed to be the Truth and then uttered falsehood, then Jesus committed sins. Claiming to be speaking the truth when you are not is a sin, a sin against truth. Your ignorance is no excuse in the face of such extravagant claims. A man who claims to be speaking with the authority of God yet does not speak the truth is judged by the Bible to be a false prophet.

We agree that Jesus was not omniscient in His human nature. But we insist that what He did teach He taught with integrity. If His teaching lacked integrity to the slightest degree, then He no longer qualifies to be anybody's Savior.

To attack Jesus' view of Scripture is to attack His integrity. If He were not sinless in His humanity He could not save Himself, let alone any of us. But we see here not only an attack on Jesus' person but an attack on His own principles of teaching. He said, "If I have told you earthly things and you do not believe, how will you believe if I tell you heavenly things?" (John 3:12).

Obviously, Jesus thought that it wasn't very wise to believe a man about heavenly matters who proved to be untrustworthy in the lesser matters of earth. Yet that is what a whole generation of Christian scholars is doing. They cling to Jesus' teaching about heaven, while denying His teaching about earthly historical matters.

This kind of modern faith violates yet another maxim of our Lord. Jesus rebuked the Pharisees for straining out the gnat and swallowing the camel. Our generation denies the inerrancy of the Bible but still affirms that Jesus is the Savior. They strain out the biblical difficulties and never have to worry again about defending the trustworthiness of Scripture. But in so doing they "swallow" a Jesus who has lost His integrity.

Because God is omniscient and Christ is infallible, we have a sure word of truth. We have a source of truth, a content of truth by which we can live with assurance. The Christian is not shackled in a dimly lit cave of ignorance or transitory opinion. We walk in the light because we have received truth from God Himself. His word, the light for our pathway, can be trusted totally.

The heavens declare the glory of God;
And the firmament shows His handiwork.
Day unto day utters speech,
And night unto night reveals knowledge.
There is no speech nor language
Where their voice is not heard.

. . . .

The law of the Lord is perfect, converting the soul;
The testimony of the Lord is sure, making wise the simple;
The statutes of the Lord are right, rejoicing the heart;
The commandment of the Lord is pure, enlightening the eyes;
The fear of the Lord is clean, enduring forever;
The judgments of the Lord are true and righteous altogether.
More to be desired are they than gold,
Yea, than much fine gold;
Sweeter also than honey and the honeycomb.
Moreover by them Your servant is warned,
And in keeping them there is great reward.
Who can understand his errors?
Cleanse me from secret faults.
Keep back Your servant also from presumptuous sins;
Let them not have dominion over me.
Then I shall be blameless,
And I shall be innocent of great transgression.
Let the words of my mouth and the meditation of my heart
Be acceptable in Your sight,
O Lord, my strength and my redeemer.

Psalm 19:1–3, 7–14

The Shadow Doesn't Turn

C. S. Lewis graced the world with uncommon Christian literature. One of his finest achievements was the creation of *The Chronicles of Narnia,* a series of children's books widely enjoyed by children—many of them over twenty-one years of age. *The Chronicles* trace the adventures of children who make an annual visit to their relatives in the countryside of England.

In the first volume, *The Lion, the Witch and the Wardrobe,* the children enter the enchanted land of Narnia via the musty environs of an old wardrobe. In Narnia the young heroine, Lucy, meets a majestic lion named Aslan. Aslan represents Christ throughout *The Chronicles.*

In the second book, when the children return to the enchanted land, they are immediately disoriented. Everything has changed radically since their first visit. The sites they used as landmarks before are now altered. Fondly remembered buildings from the previous summer are in ruins. The children quickly become lost.

After a series of dreadful events, Lucy finally meets Aslan in a forest clearing. You can almost feel her relief as she catches sight of him:

> A circle of grass, smooth as a lawn, met her eyes, with dark trees dancing all round it. And then—oh joy! For *He* was there: the huge Lion, shining white in the moonlight, with his huge black shadow underneath him.
>
> But for the movement of his tail he might have been a stone lion, but Lucy never thought of that. She never stopped to

think whether he was a friendly lion or not. She rushed to him. She felt her heart would burst if she lost a moment. And the next thing she knew was that she was kissing him and putting her arms as far round his neck as she could and burying her face in the beautiful rich silkiness of his mane.*

But then Lucy notices something about Aslan; she is shocked to see how much he had grown from the previous summer. Aslan smiles knowingly. Although only one year has passed on England's calendar, a thousand years have passed in Narnia time. He has had one thousand years to grow instead of only one; however, in spite of the long passing of time, he has not grown at all. He always stays the same size. He is the same yesterday, today, and forever.

> The great beast rolled over on his side so that Lucy fell, half sitting and half lying between his front paws. He bent forward and just touched her nose with his tongue. His warm breath came all around her. She gazed up into the large wise face.
> "Welcome, child," he said.
> "Aslan," said Lucy, "you're bigger."
> "That is because you are older, little one," answered he.
> "Not because you are?"
> "I am not. But every year you grow, you will find me bigger."*

We share Lucy's experience. When our understanding of God changes, it is not because God has changed. We are the ones who change. God doesn't grow. God doesn't improve with age. God is the Lord everlasting. He is eternally the same. He says of Himself, "For I am the LORD, I do not change" (Mal. 3:6).

To say that God does not change is to say that He is immutable—He undergoes no mutations. There is an inner consistency to the nature of God; He never goes through an inward process of evolution.

Nothing is more evident about the nature of creatures than that they change. I am a person-in-change. My weight changes from day to day. I add weight and I lose weight, but somehow it is always in an upward spiral. Changeableness is a common trait of creatures. Some of our changes are for the better, while others represent regress, a change for the worse.

*C. S. Lewis, *Prince Caspian* (New York: Macmillan, 1978), 135–136.
*Lewis, 136.

At times our changes are critical. When life hangs in the balance, we wait eagerly for reports from the hospital. We ask, "Is there any change?"

Heaven has no hospitals. God will never be named on a critical list. He does not change. He cannot get better. He does not need to improve. He is already perfect in His being. He will not deteriorate. He is not subject to the aging process. His mind never suffers from lapses of memory. He cannot forget what He eternally knows.

As human beings we change in many ways. We increase in our knowledge. We grow in grace and sanctification. We advance in wisdom. We increase in strength. These changes are possible because we are imperfect and inherently weak.

No such weakness exists in God. He is already omnipotent. That He *cannot* improve shows forth His glory and calls forth our adoration and thanksgiving. His perfection makes Him worthy of our praise. That there is no room for improvement in Him fuels our joy because we need never fear finding some hidden defect in His character.

Recently, I was playing golf on a brilliant, sunny day. Another member of the group was concentrating on a putt, and I was standing quietly out of his line of vision at the edge of the green. The man suddenly raised his head and asked me to move. I realized then to my embarrassment that my shadow had fallen over the hole making it very difficult for my friend to see his target. As I moved aside, I noticed the strange movements of my shadow. It was dancing and I found it difficult to control. As I turned, my shadow turned. As I moved, my shadow moved.

God's shadow never moves. It never moves because He has no shadow. God dwells in blazing light. His very being is the fullness of light. His glory is radiant. Even the sun that floods our planet with light has dark spots. There are no spots on God—no hint of a blemish. As the Apostle James declares: "Every good gift and every perfect gift is from above, and comes down from the Father of lights, with whom there is no variation or shadow of turning" (James 1:17).

Immutable or Immobile?

When thinking of God's immutability, it is easy to fall into the trap of conceiving God as being utterly immobilized. If

God doesn't change, does He move? Movement is a kind of change. If something never changes, must it remain static?

The Bible declares that God's unchangeableness does not mean that He is inert. God is not a rigid, fixed, stationary, paralyzed being. God is alive. He is dynamic. He is conscious.

We must affirm that God's immutability is compatible with His activity. The very concept of motion or movement is tied to space and time. Motion is only conceivable for us in material terms. We really cannot understand how a spirit "moves," particularly if that spirit is an infinite Spirit.

God's immutability, rather than implying immobility, calls attention to His internal consistency. God never stops being God. His character and His being are without diminution or augmentation; nothing can be added to or subtracted from His perfect being. God is now all that He ever was or ever shall be.

Does God Empty Himself?

A passage in the New Testament that frequently provokes debate about the character of God is the "kenotic hymn" of Philippians 2. Here the apostle speaks of a kind of kenosis or emptying that occurred in the incarnation of Christ: "Let this mind be in you which was also in Christ Jesus, who, being in the form of God, did not consider it robbery to be equal with God, but made Himself of no reputation [*emptied Himself of His privileges*], taking the form of a servant" (Phil. 2:5–7).

Great controversy has attended the use of the word *empty* in this passage. Of what did Christ empty Himself? Does this emptying threaten the truth of God's immutability?

Nineteenth-century theologians argued that Christ emptied Himself of all or some of His divine attributes when He came to Earth in the form of a man. Here the eternal Logos, the Second Person of the Trinity, laid aside His deity to join us in our humanity. This involved a kind of self-limiting act by God. At the Incarnation the immutable God changed; the infinite became finite, and the eternal became temporal. According to this view, the omniscient One suddenly found borders to His knowledge.

A common explanation for this idea is that it was necessary for God to lay aside His deity in order to understand us from a human perspective. This emptying was motivated by God's desire to identify with our human condition. It is something like a king's donning rags and living among paupers to show his compassion for them.

This explanation may seem attractive. It does emphasize that we have a friend in Jesus, One who is approachable because He has been "one of us" and understands the threats, fears, and temptations we face.

The Bible does make it clear that indeed Jesus was like us in every respect except for sin. We are encouraged to come to Him with the full assurance that He does understand our human condition. Jesus' gaining that understanding, however, did not require that He lay aside His deity. He was quite capable of understanding us fully without abandoning all or part of His divine nature.

Scripture does not teach that Jesus would have to empty Himself of His deity to understand us. This idea is not only repugnant to the Bible but repugnant to reason as well. If we pushed the point to its logical conclusion, we would be forced to say that for Jesus to be able to understand us, He must be like us. If Jesus were *fully* like us, He could not redeem us because He would also be a sinner in need of a redeemer.

The late theologian Benjamin B. Warfield once remarked that the only kenosis that actually happens in this theory is the emptying of the heads of the theologians! The crucial question is this: Can God ever cease being God? If God *is* His attributes, if He ever laid aside or emptied Himself of a single attribute, He would suddenly become less than God. This would be a mutation in God, a change in His very being. He would be mutable.

If God were not immutable, He would not be God. That which changes ceases to be what it was. That which really is, which really exists in itself, which has pure being, remains what it is. If the omniscient God emptied Himself of His omniscience, He would no longer be God. He would be a being of finite knowledge seeking to learn what He didn't know. A God who could so limit His power that He was no longer omnipotent would be a God vulnerable to extinction through the exercise of some other power in the universe.

Or suppose for a moment that God could lay aside His attributes and that in the Incarnation He, in fact, did lay them aside. What then? How would we know whether or not, at some point, He might decide to lay some other attribute aside? What would happen if five minutes before the Last Judgment God decided to empty Himself of His justice? What if He discarded His mercy? What if God decided to quit being holy?

Someone might ask, however, "Are you not limiting God in some fashion by declaring that God cannot empty Himself of His attributes and still be God?" Of course I am limiting God— limiting the use and meaning of the word *God* to that being who is God. When I say that God cannot do these things and still be God, all I am asserting is that God cannot *be* God and *not be* God at the same time. This is not a limit that I impose. It is a limit imposed by the very nature of God. God is "limited" by His own character. God cannot, does not, and will not ever act against His own nature. It is the nature of God to be immutable.

Then what exactly did God empty Himself of? Paul certainly used the word *kenosis* in Philippians 2. What the whole text of Philippians 2 makes clear is that the emptying was an emptying of divine prerogatives. Jesus laid aside His privileges. He voluntarily humbled Himself. His taking on a human nature did not subtract anything from His divine nature, but cloaked and concealed His glorious and exalted divine nature. On many occasions Jesus willingly concealed His divine authority and power. Although He warned now and then that He might call upon heaven for a display of power (summoning legions of angels, for example), in His restraint, He fulfilled the role of the obedient servant to the bitter end.

We must not forget that Jesus was, in human form, the Creator of the world. At any moment in His ministry He could have extinguished the life of those who opposed Him. The world was made by Him, in Him, and for Him. He had the power and authority to alter that creation by eliminating some undesirable rascals. But He chose to humble Himself before those very rascals. He allowed Himself to be arrested, tried, scourged, mocked, and crucified by men whom He could have annihilated with a single glance. That is humility. Acting with less power than one has at his disposal when attacked by another displays an astonishing level of grace. This is the Jesus who is our Lord. It is precisely *His* mindset that Paul called us to imitate in Philippians 2.

Can God Die?

If God is immutable, can He die? The obvious answer is no. Then why do so many Christians speak as if God could die?

Many hymns mention the death of God on the cross. Charles Wesley wrote a hymn entitled "And Can It Be" in which the lyrics express amazement and delight that our God has died for us.

Did God die on the cross? Really? Was there a moment in human history when the Lord God Omnipotent was deceased? In the darkest hour of Calvary was heaven suddenly vacant? Did God pass out of existence?

What would happen to the universe if the heart of God skipped a single beat? The universe not only was created by God but is sustained moment to moment by His power. If God were dead for one second, the world would collapse. The sun would vanish; the trees would vaporize; and no one would survive for an instant to behold it. If God died, the world would perish with Him.

Would it be better, perhaps, to say that part of God died on the cross—the Second Person of the Trinity, the divine Logos, was slain on the cross, but the world didn't perish because the Father and the Spirit were still intact? No, this is improper also. If God is three in One and only one of the three Persons died, the unity and immutability of God's essence would be destroyed. If the unity of His essence were destroyed, He would cease to be God.

Why, then, do Christians speak of God's dying on the cross? Jesus did die on the cross. Jesus was the God-man. If Jesus was God and Jesus died on the cross, it does seem logical to say God died on the cross.

Again, we must distinguish the two natures of Jesus without separating them. Human natures can die, but divine natures cannot die. Death affected Jesus' human nature. The perfect humanity of Christ was slain on the cross. That perfect humanity was in perfect union with the deity of Christ. That does not mean, however, that the deity died. The perfect union between the two natures continued even in death. The difference was that the Second Person of the Trinity was perfectly united with a human corpse rather than with a living man.

Does God Change His Mind?

If God is immutable, if He does not change at all, does that mean He never changes His mind either? This is a very thorny problem. The Bible appears to say at times that God changed His mind. Consider, for example, the following episode that took place in the time of Moses:

> Then Moses pleaded with the LORD his God, and said: "LORD, why does Your wrath burn hot against Your people whom You have brought out of the land of Egypt with great power and with a mighty hand? Why should the Egyptians speak, and say, 'He brought them out to harm them, to kill them in the mountains, and to consume them from the face of the earth'? Turn from Your fierce wrath, and relent from this harm to Your people. Remember Abraham, Isaac, and Israel, Your servants, to whom You swore by Your own self, and said to them, 'I will multiply your descendants as the stars of heaven; and all this land that I have spoken of I give to your descendants, and they shall inherit it forever.'"
> So the LORD relented from the harm which He said He would do to His people. *(Exod. 32:11–14)*

God "relented"? Other translations render the words here, "changed His mind." This narrative seems to make it absolutely clear that God does, in fact, change His mind from time to time. Maybe His being doesn't change, but does His mind cast a shadow every once in awhile?

The problem becomes more vexing when we read elsewhere in Scripture:

> "God is not a man, that He should lie,
> Nor a son of man, that He should repent.
> Has He said, and will He not do it?
> Or has He spoken, and will He not make it good?
> Behold, I have received a command to bless;
> He has blessed, and I cannot reverse it. *(Num. 23:19–20)*

This same concept is repeated elsewhere: "And also the Strength of Israel will not lie nor relent. For He is not a man, that He should relent" (1 Sam. 15:29).

Is this a contradiction in Scripture? How are we to understand this?

We could throw up our hands and agree with the Bible's critics who insist that this is a blatant error or contradiction. A more judicious approach would be to grapple with the problem of what is called phenomenological language. Scripture frequently describes events in terms of how they appear to the observer. The Bible does not "teach" that the sun revolves around the earth, but it does speak about sunrises and sunsets. (Even modern scientists do this when they are using ordinary language. Listen to what the meteorologist on your local TV station says about the sun's "rising" and "setting.")

The most obvious use of phenomenological language in the Bible is its use of human terms to describe God. The Bible speaks of His coming and of His going, of His becoming angry, of His turning from wrath. He is described as having arms, hands, a face, and feet. Yet this multitude of references to God via human imagery is qualified by sober biblical warnings and reminders that God is not a man. It is noteworthy that in these "troubling" passages the qualifier is spelled out precisely in these terms: God "is not a man that He should relent [change His mind]" (1 Sam. 15:29).

If we took the discussion between Moses and God in Exodus and pressed the apparent meaning to the ultimate, what would it teach us about God? Not only would we think that God relented, but we would think that He relented because Moses showed God a more excellent way. Is it even thinkable to us that God should have an idea that is corrected by a fallible creature? If we entertain such a thought the ramifications are sobering.

For example, in the Exodus incident Moses pleaded with God, arguing that God would look bad to the Egyptians if He carried out His threat. Then God changed His mind? Think of the meaning of this in human terms: If God first thought about punishing His people, He must have overlooked the consequence of that action on His reputation. His reasoning was flawed. His decision was impulsive. Fortunately, Moses

93

was astute enough to see the folly of this decision and persuaded the shortsighted Deity to come up with a better plan. Fortunately for God, He was helped by a superior guidance counselor. Without the help of Moses, God would have made a foolish mistake!

Even to talk like this is to border on blasphemy. That God could be corrected by Moses or any other creature is utterly unthinkable. Yet, that seems to be the implication of the narrative. This is a major reason why we must interpret the narrative passages of Scripture by the didactic or "teaching" portions. If we try to find too much theology in narrative passages, we can easily go beyond the point of the narrative into serious errors.

The biblical narratives in which God appears to repent, or change His mind, are almost always narratives that deal with His threats of judgment and punishment. These threats are then followed by the repentance of the people or by the intercessory petitions of their leaders. God is not talked into "changing His mind." Out of His gracious heart He only does what He has promised to do all along—not punish sinners who repent and turn from their evil ways. He chooses not to do what He has every right to do.

The point of these narratives is to encourage us to pray. We are to make intercession. The promised threats of divine punishment are given with the condition attached that if we repent, we will escape those punishments. Sometimes that condition is spelled out explicitly, while at other times it is merely implied. When we repent, then God removes the threat of punishment. The question is, Who is ultimately repenting here? God never repents in the sense that He turns away from sin or from error.

God is not a man. He does not ultimately or literally have arms or legs. He does not repent as men repent. He listens to our prayers but is never corrected by them. He changes not—neither in the perfection of His being nor in the perfection of His thoughts.

Does God Learn Things?

Closely related to the question of God's changing His mind is the question of God's knowledge. Are there gaps in His omniscience that need to be filled? Obviously, to ask that question in the manner I have is to answer it. If there were gaps in God's knowledge, we could no longer speak of His omniscience.

Some biblical texts, however, suggest that God is still learning things.

Consider the narrative of Abraham at Mount Moriah: "And He said, 'Do not lay your hand on the lad, or do anything to him; for now I know that you fear God, seeing you have not withheld your son, your only son, from Me'" (Gen. 22:12).

Does this suggest that God educated Himself when He said "now I know"? Was God wondering the whole time if Abraham would or would not grasp the knife and plunge it into his son's body? One answer might be that these words were said by an angel of God to Abraham and not by God Himself. There is obviously nothing wrong with angels learning things because angels are not omniscient. Though the words are spoken by an angel, however, they are the words of God. The angel is a messenger; he speaks God's words to Abraham.

There is more to this question than what may meet the eye. Lurking in the background is a major theological controversy: Does God know the future actions of free people?

Before looking at that very serious issue, what about the case of Abraham at Mount Moriah? If God knew in advance what Abraham was going to do, why did He say, "now I know"? It seems obvious that God did not know in advance. Can we not picture the Deity wringing His hands in heaven, waiting anxiously for moment-to-moment bulletins on the progress of His servant Abraham? Can we imagine God sighing in relief when the news reached Him that Abraham had been obedient—happy now that He could get on with His plan of redemption? Can we imagine God going through the same agony while waiting for the results of the Fall or Jesus' temptation in the wilderness? If God does not know the future free choices of men, how could He possibly predict them with accuracy in prophecy?

The fact that God can and does predict the future actions of people in perfect detail indicates that He has foreknowledge. The Bible speaks directly of this foreknowledge both by using the word itself and by expressing the concept. God knew what

Judas would do before he did it. Jesus' ability to predict the betrayals of both Judas and Peter reflects this type of foreknowledge.

Does Human Freedom Exist?

Does God's foreknowledge eliminate human freedom? Does the immutability of God and the omniscience of God mean the end of all human freedom? If free human actions were not known in advance by God, then when He learned of them, He would undergo a change in His knowledge; He would learn something new. Here both immutability and omniscience would be compromised.

If human actions are known by God in advance, is it not certain that they will come to pass exactly as God has foreknown them? If God knows today what I will do tomorrow, then there is no doubt that when tomorrow comes, I will do what God already knows I will do. With respect to the mind of God my future behavior is absolutely certain. But, does that mean that my future actions are absolutely determined or coerced by God?

God can know the future in more than one way. He can know the future because He has determined the future, or He can know it as a spectator. Consider the following analogy. Suppose you are standing at the corner of the roof atop a five-story building. As you look down to the street directly below, you see two runners on the sidewalk. One of them is approaching the edge of the building below you from south to north. The other runner is approaching the edge from west to east. They cannot see each other because their view is obscured by the building. From where you are standing you can see that the two runners are going to collide. You want to shout for them to stop, but you know it is too late. They are a split second away from crashing into each other. All you can do is stand helplessly waiting for the collision.

The analogy suggests a human way of knowing the future without causing or forcing the future to happen. (Of course, like any analogy, it is far from perfect. It is possible that one of the runners will step into a manhole just before he reaches the corner, or one might be vaporized by a laser gun at the last second. Our knowledge of the future in this case is not really certain.) The point of the analogy, though, is simply to illustrate that we can have knowledge of future events without causing those future events.

Some have approached the subject of God's foreknowledge from a different perspective. Their argument is based on God's relationship to space and time. The idea is this: God is eternal; He is above space and time. God sees all things from the vantage point of the present. There is no past or future with God. He sees all things as present. If God sees all things as present, then how He does it is completely beyond our comprehension. What God's ultimate relationship to time is remains a highly speculative matter. If what is future to me is present to God, then we know His knowledge of our future is perfect and that future is absolutely certain. God can make no errors in His observations.

It is one thing to say that God causes or coerces all things. It is quite another to say that God foreordains all things. If God forces or coerces all things, then He would have had to coerce the fall of man. If this were so, then God would be the cause, indeed the guilty perpetrator of sin. Not only would God be guilty of sin but His coercive actions would destroy the freedom of man.

To aid understanding we need to consider two models, two images of God, which lead to serious distortions of the divine character. First is the image of God as a puppeteer. Here God manipulates the strings of marionettes. The feet and the arms of the puppets jerk and dance as God pulls the strings. Puppets have no will. They have no heart or soul. Their bodies are filled with sawdust. If God were like this, not even the Wizard of Oz could make us truly free.

The second image of God is of the spectator. Here God sits on the sidelines of world history. He observes the game closely. He makes careful notes about the action and will turn in a scouting report. He is the ultimate armchair quarterback. He second-guesses the plays that are called. He roots for His favorite team. However, He is powerless to affect the outcome of the game in any way. The action is on the field, and He's not playing. This model of God destroys His sovereignty. The spectator God is a God who reigns but never rules. He is a God without authority. He observes history but is not Lord over history.

Neither of these images does justice to the biblical view of God. They serve merely to alert us to the pitfalls that lurk in the shadows. They represent borders over which we must not go.

We must be careful not to so zealously maintain the sovereignty of God that we end up denying human freedom and responsibility. At the same time we must be careful not to so zealously preserve human freedom that we reduce God to an impotent spectator of world affairs.

The correct approach is to insist that God foreordains all things and that all future events are under His sovereignty. The future is absolutely certain to God. He knows what will take place, and He foreordains what will take place. *Foreordain* does not mean coerce. It simply means that God wills that something take place. He may will future events through the free choices of creatures. This is the great mystery of providence—that God can will the means as well as the ends of future events. God can even will good through the wicked choices of men.

The greatest event of human history was at the same time the most diabolical. No greater shame can be tacked to the human race than that a human being delivered up Jesus to be crucified. Judas betrayed Christ because Judas wanted to betray Christ. The Pharisees pressed for His death because the Pharisees wanted Jesus killed. Pilate succumbed to the howling crowd, not because God coerced him, but because Pilate was too weak to withstand the demands of the mob.

Yet the Bible declares that the Cross was no accident. The outcome of God's eternal plan of redemption did not hinge finally on the decision of Pontius Pilate. What if Pilate had released Jesus and crucified Barabbas instead? Such a thought is almost unthinkable. It would suggest that God was only a spectator in the plan of redemption, that He hoped for the best but had no control over the events.

God did more than hope for the Cross. He willed the Cross. He sent His Son for that very purpose. Before Jesus was brought before Pilate, He pleaded with the Father for a different verdict. He begged that the cup might pass. Before Pilate ever raised his Roman scepter, the gavel had fallen in

Gethsemane. The verdict was in. Jesus was delivered by the determinate forecounsel of God.

Augustine said that "In a certain sense God wills everything that comes to pass." He ordains things with a view to human freedom. He does no violence to our wills by His sovereign ordination. He is not a spectator and we are not puppets. His knowledge is certain, and our actions are free.

How the providence of God works out these matters of concurrence is mysterious but not contradictory. There is nothing that is rationally incompatible about God's sovereignty and human freedom. Scripture clearly teaches that God is sovereign and that man is responsible. Neither teaching is false. I am not proposing that freedom and sovereignty are not contradictions simply because the Bible teaches both. I am saying that the two concepts are not contradictory because they are not mutually exclusive concepts. Divine sovereignty and human autonomy would be mutually exclusive. If God is sovereign man could not be autonomous. If man is autonomous God could not be sovereign.

God is sovereign. Man is free. Man's freedom is limited, however, by God's sovereignty. God's sovereignty is not limited by man's freedom. This is simply to say that man is not God. God is free and man is free. But God is more free than man. Man's freedom is always and everywhere subordinate to God's freedom. If we reverse these we pass from theism to atheism, from Christianity to humanism, from Christ to Antichrist.

God in Process

Scholars of the modern era have written much about a God-in-process. Modern thinkers have flirted heavily with a finite God, a God who is a part of the process of change, growth, and development. Images of a God who Himself must work through certain internal struggles abound in modern literature. Such views do not hesitate to deny the immutability of God. The finite God is marred by an ever turning shadow. He is a chameleon. He may not be tomorrow what He is today.

The late Swiss theologian Emil Brunner made the following comment about a changing God:

The fact that God shares in what happens upon earth does not, in any sense, mean that idea which is so dear to modern man: the God who "becomes." The idea of a "God who becomes" is a mythological and unreal idea. Were God Himself One who is "becoming" then everything would flounder in the morass of relativism. We can measure nothing by changing standards; changing norms are no norms at all; a God who is constantly changing is not a God whom we can worship, He is a mythological Being for whom we can only feel sorry. The God of the Bible is eternally unchangeable.*

Brunner declared that a changing God would result in changing norms and changing norms are no norms at all. A changing norm would be merely a passing fancy, a temporary preference.

We live in a society where cliches such as laws are made to be broken abound. Such a sentiment can be translated, "Norms are made to be changed." This is the new ethic, the ethic of relativism. Upon examination, however, we find that the ethic is not new at all. It had its advocate in Eden: Laws are made to be broken was the maxim of the serpent.

Is the "modern" idea of changing norms the result of a shift in our understanding of a God who is immutable to a God-in-process, or is the God-in-process notion the result of our shift in ethics? If mankind dares to tamper with the law of God, that tampering must be justified. Nothing suits the cause of revising the ethics of God better than redefining the nature of God.

When we transgress the law of God, we are left with three chief options: 1) We can repent, which involves change in us. 2) We can redefine the basis of ethics to meet our level of behavior. 3) We can redefine the character of God to make Him less threatening to us. The latter two options are less painful to us than repentance.

This is the essence of idolatry, to change the immutable God into something less than He is. Idolatry is as foolish to God as it is repugnant. We can change our concept of God. We can change our theology. We can change our attitude toward God.

*Emil Brunner, The Christian Doctrine of God, trans. by Olive Wyon (Philadelphia: Westminster Press, 1980), p. 269.

The Lord reigns,
He is clothed with majesty;
The Lord is clothed,
He has girded Himself with strength.
Surely the world is established, so that it cannot be moved.
Your throne is established from of old;
You are from everlasting.
The floods have lifted up, O Lord,
The floods have lifted up their voice;
The floods lift up their waves.
The Lord on high is mightier
Than the noise of many waters,
Than the mighty waves of the sea.
Your testimonies are very sure;
Holiness adorns Your house,
O Lord, forever.

Psalm 93

But one thing we cannot do: We cannot change God. God is unchangeable.

If changes are to be made, they must be made in us.

CHAPTER VIII

THE JUST JUDGE

Diogenes, the Greek philosopher, was famous for two things. First, it is rumored that he lived in a bathtub and took his tub with him wherever he went, looking like a human turtle. His second and more important possession was a lamp. With his lamp he searched every nook and cranny of ancient Athens, looking for an honest man. Again, rumor has it that his lamp wore out before he was able to attain success. His search was futile.

The Bible says of mankind that none is righteous, no, not one (see Rom. 3:10). A million Diogenes, armed with an equal number of lamps, could search the entire world without finding a perfectly righteous person. If we are to find the One who is righteous, we must aim our lamps toward heaven, the only place where the righteous dwell.

This is THE dilemma: On earth there is an absence of perfect righteousness; in heaven there is a fullness of righteousness. Because God is righteous and we are not, we need a Savior. A righteous God requires righteousness from His creatures. If we fail to provide our own, then we must look elsewhere to secure it. Our search is desperate and futile unless we turn our attention from Athens to Jerusalem. There we can uncover the story of the alien who visited this planet as a mysterious stranger bearing a mysterious gift. His gift was His own righteousness, which He gave to those who put their trust in

Him and in Him alone. Christ is our righteousness. He is the righteous One.

What Is Righteousness?

Righteousness is not an easy concept to define in spite of its being so oft-mentioned in Scripture. In the Bible the idea of God's righteousness is closely related to His holiness and justice.

Righteousness. Holiness. Justice. These three key words are so closely linked an extrasharp razor is required to distinguish them. Let's begin with the word *holy*. The biblical concept of holiness has two primary meanings: The first meaning is simply "apartness" or "separateness." That which is holy is set apart from common things. It is different; it is *other*. To say that God is Other is to say He transcends the entire creation. His august majesty is incomparable. The splendor of His glory has no analogy in creation. He is singular and unique in His exaltation. This is a far different kind of apartness from the unholy "apartheid" made infamous in South Africa.

The secondary meaning of God's holiness refers to His purity. There is no moral blemish, no defect, no stain of wickedness to mar His character. He is the Lion without blemish who reigns and rules with purity.

The holiness of God is linked to the righteousness of God in this way: With respect to God, we distinguish between His internal righteousness and His external righteousness, or more simply, what God is and what God does. His external righteousness is revealed by His actions. God does righteous acts because He is righteous. God can only act consistently with who He is.

The biblical concept of righteousness is rooted in a Hebrew word that literally means "straight." Interestingly, even today this concrete image is used as a metaphor for good and proper conduct. When a criminal reforms his life, he "goes straight." When a person wants to live an obedient life, he walks the "straight and narrow." A person who is well-behaved rather than unruly is "straight." Conversely, if someone is dishonest, he is "crooked."

To be righteous is simply to do what is right. From a human standpoint, righteousness is obedience to the law of God. That poses a difficult problem in understanding God's righteousness, as we will see later.

God's righteousness is linked, too, to the biblical concept of justice. God is at once righteous and just. The two concepts are so closely connected that, though they can be distinguished, they may not be separated. In biblical terms true justice is always "according to righteousness." Justice is not determined merely by an abstract legal code nor even by the collective decisions of the law courts. Justice is weighed by the standard of righteousness, which in turn is measured by the standard of God's character.

Must God "Obey the Law"?

God measures our righteousness by God's law. His law and our traditions do not always match up. That is why it is urgent in every generation for Christians to search the Scriptures to see if the rules by which they live are the rules of God and not merely the rules of men.

By what rules does God live? How is God's righteousness measured? Is there a law above God to which God is held accountable? These questions have been the subject of much debate in church history.

We can state the question another way. Are God's actions right simply because it is God who does them? Since He is the ultimate standard of righteousness, doesn't that mean that what He chooses to do is right no matter what? The thinly veiled dilemma here is if God did something "bad," would it really be bad?

Lurking behind such theoretical questions are two concerns. First, is there something "out there" that is higher than God? If there is some independent norm or law of righteousness that God must obey and by which He is judged, it would seem that this superimportant, independent law would be higher than God. If there is something out there higher than God, no longer should God be called "God." The higher reality would have to be God.

The second concern flows from the first. If there is not some objective, independent law out there by which God is judged, then it would seem God could be arbitrary and still be righteous. No moral standard would hold God accountable. He could do whatever pleased Him and we would have to say that it is good, even if an action violated God's own moral law.

The truth is that God is neither under law nor apart from law but rather is a law unto Himself. God's actions are bound by God's nature. He always must act and does act according to His own character. His own character is altogether pure and morally perfect. He cannot act in an arbitrary manner because it is not His nature to be arbitrary.

No law is higher than the internal character of God. God Himself is the *summmum bonum*. He is the canon of all perfection, the norm of all ethics, the fountainhead of all goodness. There is nothing higher than God, because there can be nothing higher than God.

The Bible says of God: "Shall not the Judge of all the earth do right?" (Gen. 18:25). This is a rhetorical question than can have only one answer, "Yes!" Of course the Judge of all the earth will do right. That is the only thing the Judge of all the earth knows how to do. He is morally incapable of doing anything less than what is right.

A man whom Scripture refers to as the "Father of the faithful," Abraham, once asked God a question. Abraham was living in Sodom, a wicked city God wanted to destroy. Abraham inquired, would God destroy the righteous along with the wicked?

> "Suppose there were fifty righteous within the city; would You also destroy the place and not spare it for the fifty righteous that were in it? Far be it from You to do such a thing as this, to slay the righteous with the wicked, . . . far be it from You! Shall not the Judge of all the earth do right?"
>
> *(Gen. 18:24–25)*

Punishing the righteous along with the wicked is an unjust act used not by God but by unjust judges. Who can forget our childhood rage and fury when the teacher kept the whole class from recess because of the actions of a single unknown culprit? This use of extortion would turn the entire class into a posse of vigilantes by punishing everyone for the sins of an individual. For many of us this became our first taste of the reality of unjust judgment in this world.

We see the crucial importance of God's unfailing righteousness in God's role as Judge of all the earth. What a great comfort to know that the Judge of all the earth is a righteous Judge. What madness it would be, what despair it would provoke to discover that the Judge of all the earth was not righteous.

Kant's Moral Argument

Immanuel Kant is famous for his massive critique of the traditional arguments for the existence of God. What he banished from the front door, however, he welcomed in through the back door. Though Kant was skeptical about the theoretical proofs for the existence of God, he formulated a practical argument for God's existence.

In simplified form Kant said: If ethics are to be meaningful, we must live "as if" there is a God. In other words, if there is no God, human ethics are meaningless. Dostoevsky expressed a similar sentiment: "If there is no God then all things are permissible."

How did Kant come to this conclusion? He observed that injustices occurred in this world. He noticed the type of thing King David inquired of—"Why do the righteous suffer and the wicked prosper?"

Next, Kant asked what would be necessary for ultimate justice to take place. Since perfect justice does not take place in this world, there must be some kind of life after death where justice can be executed. That means simply that we must survive the grave.

But surviving the grave will not alone guarantee that justice will be done. The future world may bring as much injustice as this world. Therefore, there must be some kind of judgment whereby justice is decreed and carried out. For that to happen we must have a Judge.

What must the Judge be like to guarantee perfect justice? First of all the Judge must be just, or He might become an instrument of injustice. But what if He is just in Himself but is ignorant of all the facts in the case? A just judge could make a legitimate mistake and accidentally miscarry justice. Therefore, the Judge must be both just and omniscient. He must know every subtle nuance of every case if He is to insure perfect justice.

If the Judge is perfect in His knowledge and perfect in His justice, will that insure justice? No. Not yet. It is possible to conceive of an omniscient, perfectly righteous Judge who is powerless to carry out His decrees. To insure perfect justice the perfect Judge must be omnipotent—able to guarantee that justice is done.

Behind all this is the question, If there is no God, why should I be concerned about justice or righteousness? If the wicked prosper and the righteous often suffer, why would anyone ever desire righteousness? To hunger and thirst after righteousness would be an exercise for fools. Yet, Kant realized that what is at stake here is not merely religion but civilization itself. Without a meaningful basis for ethics, human civilization cannot survive; it is left with arbitrary traditions that have no moral suasion to them. The final ethic in such a world is the intolerable, brutally real ethic of might makes right—the ethic of gun barrels.

Kant was by no means the only philosopher to address these problems. The issue had also been addressed by Jesus in one of His most important parables.

The Unjust Judge

Luke introduces the parable of the unjust judge by saying that "Men always ought to pray and not lose heart" (Luke 18:1). What is it that causes men to lose heart? The experience of injustice. Few things grieve the human soul more bitterly than the taste of injustice. It is one thing to feel the lash of the whip when we are guilty; but to be victims of punishment when we are innocent is exceedingly difficult to bear. Here we can identify with the thief on the cross who said, "Do you not even fear God, seeing you are under the same condemnation? And we indeed justly, for we receive the due reward of our deeds; but this Man has done nothing wrong" (Luke 23:40–41).

Surely, the spirit of Christ was moved by the thief's acknowledgment that Jesus was suffering unjustly at the hands of men. The thief accepted the justness of his own punishment but recognized the innocence of Jesus. To suffer unjustly is to be pushed to the rim of despair. Jesus' parable addresses the problem:

> "There was in a certain city a judge who did not fear God nor regard man. Now there was a widow in that city; and she came to him, saying, 'Avenge me of my adversary.' And he would not for a while; but afterward he said within himself, 'Though I do not fear God nor regard man, yet because this widow troubles me I will avenge her, lest by her continual coming she weary me.'"
>
> Then the Lord said, "Hear what the unjust judge said. And shall God not avenge His own elect who cry out day and night to Him, though He bears long with them? I tell you that He will avenge them speedily. Nevertheless, when the Son of Man comes, will He really find faith on the earth?"
>
> *(Luke 18:2–8)*

Here we find an unqualified promise from Jesus: The injustices of this world will be rectified. He declares that though God forbears injustices in this world, He ultimately will establish justice. The righteous Judge of all the earth hears the cries of His people. He is not an unjust judge. He does not turn away from the pleas of the helpless. God does not respond to bribes or hear only the cases of the rich and powerful. He does not allow Lady Justice to peek from beneath her blindfold. The Judge of all the earth is no respecter of persons. With Him there is no partiality. His scales are in balance.

The text of this parable as I have presented it from the New King James Bible speaks of God's avenging His people. An alternate word, *vindicate*, is sometimes used instead of avenge. Though the terms *avenge* and *vindicate* are closely related, they are not synonyms. *Webster's New Collegiate Dictionary* defines the word *avenge*, "to exact satisfaction for a wrong by punishing the wrongdoer." The term *vindicate* has the chief meaning of "to absolve or to exonerate." An innocent verdict vindicates the accused of the charge against him.

111

I stress this point because God, as the perfect Judge, promises both to vindicate and to avenge. He will exonerate those who are victims of slander and false accusation. Our Lord declared, "Blessed are you when they revile and persecute you, and say all kinds of evil against you falsely for My sake. Rejoice and be exceedingly glad, for great is your reward in heaven, for so they persecuted the prophets who were before you" (Matt. 5:11–12).

I had a traumatic experience while a seminary student. In my senior year, I was asked to address the faculty and the student body in a morning chapel. I chose to speak on the biblical concept of sin. Afterward, I was confronted by three faculty members who were incensed by what I had said. They accused me of seriously distorting the biblical view of sin. I thought I had presented the classical Christian view on the matter, but the reaction of such learned and respected professors threw me into a tizzy. Hurt and confused, I left the chapel and visited the professor of church history, whom I regarded as the chief seminary expert on theological orthodoxy. I told him what had happened and asked him if I had distorted the Scriptures. He replied with a broad smile, "You are very fortunate, indeed."

"Why do you say that?" I asked, shocked by his words.

The professor replied, "Because what you said was pure, unadulterated biblical Christianity. Every saint from Augustine to B. B. Warfield is rejoicing over your sermon this morning. You are fortunate because our Lord promised a special reward for those who are reviled for His sake. That is what just happened to you."

I took great comfort from those words. Every Christian has had multiple experiences of the same order. Personal attacks like that are so painful and intimidating that we are tempted not to speak boldly for Christ again. We must know with full assurance that such episodes do not escape God's eye. He has promised vindication, plus the benefit of reward.

God also promises vengeance. "'Vengeance is Mine, I will repay,' says the Lord" (Rom. 12:19). Because God forbids us from carrying out vengeance, we easily leap to the conclusion that vengeance is evil. On the contrary, vengeance is an expression of justice. God uses civil magistrates as instruments of vengeance in bringing about justice, but vengeance still *belongs* to Him.

If vengeance were intrinsically evil, then it would be as wicked for God to exact vengeance as it is for us to seek it ourselves. If it is not evil, why then is it forbidden to us? When revenge is carried beyond the level of what is just, it is evil. That is, if the punishment is more severe than the crime, then the punishment itself becomes a crime, an act of injustice. If you or I seek our own revenge, the tendency will be to overreact, to enact more than vengeance. We will not be satisfied with getting even; we will press to go one up. That is the stuff that feuds are made of. The Hatfields and the McCoys knew all about self-appointed acts of vengeance.

When God avenges, His vengeance is just. God never punishes more severely than the crime deserves.

The Government's Role in Justice

God's justice is an expression of God's righteousness, and justice sometimes may be administered directly and immediately by God's divine providence. But the normal and regular vehicle of divine justice is a mediator. God has appointed the state to be His instrument of justice.

> For rulers are not a terror to good works, but to evil. Do you want to be unafraid of the authority? Do what is good, and you will have praise from the same. For he is God's minister to you for good. But if you do evil, be afraid; for he does not bear the sword in vain; for he is God's minister, an avenger to execute wrath on him who practices evil. *(Rom. 13:3–4)*

The government is created by God and called of God to be a minister. To enter government service is to enter a "ministry." A government does not rule by its own authority; its authority is derived and dependent. Its use of power is symbolized by the sword. God puts the sword in the hands of the civil government. That sword, however, is never, never to be used as an instrument of tyranny. It is an instrument for enforcing justice.

113

The justice God commands the state to uphold is not an arbitrary justice but a justice according to righteousness. Here is where governments falter; at this point, the legislative system of the United States gets in serious trouble. Laws are to express, maintain, and promote justice. Every law of every society will be judged by God's standard of righteousness. The justness of a law can never be determined by a majority vote or even by a court of nine judges. Ultimately, a law is just or unjust based on its conformity to the character of God.

If the voter or the lawyer or the legislator or the judge deals with the law simply in terms of expediency or vested interests, then the law will inevitably be distorted. To be sure some laws passed out of vested interest do conform to justice. Such fortunate accidents are a mixed blessing, though, for with each one of them comes a growing public acceptance of a system of law based upon something other than justice.

Recently I was asked to address a group of congressional staff persons in Washington, D.C., who are Christians. I made the point that we need people in government who are more interested in the next generation than in the next election. I pleaded for Christians in Congress to vote according to what is right rather than according to what is politically expedient.

After my speech I asked for questions and discussion. Explaining the harsh realities of political survival, one staff person said, "Unless my boss [a U.S. Senator] is willing to compromise for the next several months until the election is over, he will surely lose. If we want Christians to stay in office, they must compromise during an election year so that we will be able to continue for another term."

"What I hear you saying," I replied, "is that in order for us to have the advantage of a man of integrity over the long haul, that man must sacrifice his integrity over the short haul. That is precisely the kind of person I want to get rid of in government. Give me a pagan with a conscience any day over that kind of Christian."

The unjust judge of Jesus' parable was not quite as corrupt as some of our contemporary judges. The parable says that he had no regard either for God or for man. We have plenty of jurists today who have no time for God, but there are few who have no regard for man. That is the problem. They have too much regard for man. They are not overcommitted to the dignity or needs of man. Rather, their concern is for the political approval of man.

The vote can be a precious or a vicious thing. Designed to be used as an instrument of justice, the vote can easily become a club of injustice. Tyranny is not restricted to autocracies; democracies can tyrannize through the rule of the crowd over the individual. I will never have the moral right to vote for what is wrong; I do have the legal right to vote for what is wrong.

What is the difference between a moral and a legal right? A legal right is permitted by the civil law. A moral right is permitted by the moral law of God. They are not always the same. The state might allow me to do something that God forbids or forbid me from doing something that God commands.

Mindless Christianity (which is no Christianity) accepts the legal status quo as the moral law of God. This can happen and does happen among conservatives and liberals alike. As civil laws change, so do the behavioral patterns of a culture. We can argue about whether the behavior changes first and then is legitimized by changes in the law or the opposite. Both syndromes occur.

Consider abortion. Twenty years ago abortion was a major crime in America. For the mainstream of the culture, it was also an unthinkable act. Only a small minority of people practiced or approved of it. Today it is a multimillion dollar enterprise—about one and one-half million legal abortions are performed every year. According to opinion polls, about fifty percent of the population either approves of abortion or at least approves the legal right of abortion. How could such a radical change in the moral approval of such an action have taken place in such a short period of time?

The answer is complex, and there were several factors—one of the more crucial being the pro-abortionists' understanding the brilliance of the "divide and conquer" strategy. They understood decades ago that to change the opinion on abortion in this country would require a daring move. They found one. Consciously, they created a third alternative between the two polar opposites of pro-abortion and pro-life—the option of pro-choice. Pro-choice is a middle ground, a comfortable place for nonextremists to stand. It is a position whose virtues are easily seen as pro-freedom and antimoral coercion. The person who votes for pro-choice does not have to approve of abortion but merely approves of freedom.

The pro-abortionists knew there were more people in favor of freedom than in favor of abortion. If they aligned with those who were pro-freedom, they might have a chance to change the cultural patterns. They also found another popular link-up with the growing sentiment for the liberation of women.

The pro-abortionists realized one crucial point: Although there is a major philosophical difference between being pro-abortion and pro-choice, there is no legal difference between them. A vote for pro-choice is a vote for pro-abortion. By mobilizing the middle of the road in America and by giving a popular, nonextremist alternative to pro-abortion, the pro-abortionists were able to overthrow the cultural opposition to their platform.

We see the confusion between moral rights and legal rights in the pro-abortionists' claim that "Every woman has a right to her own body." The question is, What kind of right are we talking about? A legal right? A moral right? If a person argues for the legal right, the argument is circular. At issue is not what the law of the state already is but what the law of the state ought to be. Clearly the woman now has the legal right to abortion. The debate rages over whether or not she ought to have such a right.

When a person declares that abortion is fine because a woman has a right to her own body, the assumption is that this is her moral right. But where does the woman get such a moral right? Does she get it from God? If so, where do we find any evidence that God has given her such a right? If a woman has a moral right over her own body, then every woman has the moral right to be a harlot or the inherent moral right to suicide.

The Scriptures make it clear that neither men nor women have any absolute moral right over their own bodies. On the contrary, divine laws mandate personal responsibility for the well-being of our physical bodies.

That a woman has a moral right to her own body is a vacuous and specious argument. What the statement really asserts, in an indirect way, is that women have a right to do what they desire, whatever turns them on.

If there is a God, and if that God is righteous, then no creature under His righteous authority ever has the right to do wrong. Here the righteousness of God explodes on the scene of human ethical behavior. There is nothing remote or abstract about the righteousness of God. It has everything to do with what we do. His righteousness is the ultimate standard of our behavior, of our laws, and of our lives.

Conscience is often shaped by the mores of our culture, and an unthinking person may accept as "right" whatever is the prevailing morality. No Christian can afford to do that. With every vote and every law and every behavioral choice, we must ask the question, Is it right?

The Justification Controversy

The righteousness of God is at the very heart of the Christian life. There can be no Christian life without it. We enter the Christian life by the door of justification. If we are not justified we are not Christian. No one who is not justified will ever inherit the kingdom of God. Justification is a *sine qua non* of Christianity.

It is no accident that the greatest controversy in the history of the Christian church centered on the question of justification. Because of this issue the church of Christ fragmented into thousands of individual pieces. Theologians have fussed and debated over a host of lesser issues, but the protest of the Protestant Reformation was not over trifles. The issue was worthy of great controversy because it had eternal consequences. *The* issue of the Reformation was How is a person redeemed?

Justification is at the heart of the Christian faith because (1) God is righteous, and (2) man is not righteous. These two facts make Christianity necessary and stand behind the Incarnation, the Cross, the empty tomb. If God were not righteous, unrighteous human beings would have no need of a Savior. But because God is righteous and we are not, we have a desperate need for a Savior.

How could unjust people stand before the judgment throne of a just and righteous God? They could not unless they were first justified. That last sentence is precisely the sentence that the vast majority of Americans have never grasped. Most folks will agree that God is righteous. Most will agree that human beings are not righteous or at least not perfectly righteous. But this disparity between the righteousness of God and our unrighteousness does not seem to bother many people because they assume it is really not a serious matter. God may be righteous, but He is also merciful, so we don't have much to worry about. God is well known for clearing the guilty.

God does have that reputation. I once administered a theological examination to a group of about one hundred ministers. Part of the test was a true/false section. One of the questions asked: True or False—The only way God will ever clear the guilty is by the atonement of Jesus Christ.

How did you answer the question? Every one of the ministers answered "True." They were all wrong; the answer is false. There is no way that God *clears* the guilty. He justifies the guilty through Christ. To clear the guilty would be to declare a guilty person innocent. That is one thing God will never do. God does justify the ungodly; He saves us while we are still sinners.

The gospel declares that we are justified by faith, which means in its simplest terms that we are justified by Christ. To be justified by Christ is to receive the imputation of His righteousness. Once I receive His righteousness then God declares me just. He will not make that declaration a moment before I receive the righteousness of Christ, nor does He hesitate for a second after I receive it.

One of the deepest points of Roman Catholic criticism against Protestant theology is that the doctrine of justification by faith alone is a "legal fiction," that is, it involves God in declaring people just who are not in fact just. Rome reacted vigorously against Luther's statement that the justified man is at the same time just and sinner. What Luther meant was that a justified sinner considered by himself is still a sinner. But God does not consider him in and of himself. God sees the imputed righteousness of Christ. What Rome failed to understand in Luther's formula is that the imputation of the righteousness of Christ to the believing sinner is a real imputation. By faith we really and actually possess the righteousness of Jesus. That is why we are really and actually justified.

God meets the deficiency in our righteousness by supplying us with righteousness from someone else. Herein is our salvation, that Jesus has taken my guilt and given to me His righteousness. Because we are clothed in the righteousness of Christ, we will be able to survive the Last Judgment. Without that righteousness we would surely perish, for God would not abandon or in any way compromise His righteousness in order to save you and me.

Reward and Punishment

A just judge is one who gives proper rewards for righteousness and proper punishments for evil. God's justice is both *remunerative* and *distributive*. He remunerates good works and distributes punishments for evil works. In the Old Testament God gave His law to the people of Israel. With the Law came dual sanctions, two options of Divine response to the people's performance—blessings and curses:

> "Now it shall come to pass, if you diligently obey the voice of the LORD your God, to observe carefully all His commandments which I command you today, that the LORD your God will set you high above all nations of the earth. And all these blessings shall come upon you and overtake you, because you obey the voice of the LORD your God: Blessed shall you be in the city, and blessed shall you be in the country. Blessed shall be the fruit of your body, the produce of your ground, and the increase of your herds, the increase of your cattle and the offspring of your flocks. Blessed shall be your basket and your kneading bowl. Blessed shall you be when you come in, and blessed shall you be when you go out." *(Deut. 28:1–6)*

The promise of blessing is given for obedience. This is not the same concept as a strict merit system where works that are so praiseworthy morally obligate a just judge to reward them. However, the good works of a fallen sinner are always at least partially tainted by sin. Thus, God is never obligated by the strict rules of justice to reward any of our actions.

Yet, God promises to reward our efforts. How are we to understand this? Here we see an example of *de pacto* reward. The idea is that God makes a pact or an agreement with us. He promises to reward us if we do certain things. The reward itself is gracious. He is under no obligation to make the promise in the first place. His promise comes from His mercy. Once He makes the promise, however, He is consistent with His word; He will keep His promise and give the reward.

The New Testament is full of promises of rewards that will be distributed in heaven according to our works. I often ask my students the following true/false question: True or False— Justification is by faith alone, but our reward in heaven will be distributed according to our works. Many earnest Protestant students stumble over this question, but the correct Protestant answer is "True." The words "according to" are crucial to our understanding.

Saint Augustine made the famous statement that in giving us rewards, God was, in fact, "crowning His own gifts." He meant that the only way we can perform any measure of obedience to God is by God's merciful help. Not only does He stoop to help us, but He then rewards us for what we couldn't possibly have done without His help.

The dark side to the pact God made with His people is that there are serious consequences for those who do not obey the law of God:

> "But it shall come to pass, if you do not obey the voice of the LORD your God, to observe carefully all His commandments and His statutes which I command you today, that all these curses will come upon you and overtake you: Cursed shall you be in the city, and cursed shall you be in the country. Cursed shall be your basket and your kneading bowl. Cursed shall be the fruit of your body and the produce of your land, the increase of your cattle and the offspring of your flocks. Cursed shall you be when you come in, and cursed shall you be when you go out. *(Deut. 28:15–19)*

The promise of the curse of God is the promise of His just wrath against the works of disobedience. Here we see the distributive justice of God. The just Judge must punish evil. This concept is at the very core of our redemption. God

Praise the Lord!
I will praise the Lord with my whole heart,
In the assembly of the upright and in the congregation.
The works of the Lord are great,
Studied by all who have pleasure in them.
His work is honorable and glorious,
And His righteousness endures forever.
He has made His wonderful works to be remembered;
The Lord is gracious and full of compassion.
He has given food to those who fear Him;
He will ever be mindful of His covenant.
He has declared to His people the power of His works,
In giving them the heritage of the nations.
The works of His hands are verity and justice;
All His precepts are sure.
They stand fast forever and ever,
And are done in truth and uprightness.
He has sent redemption to His people;
He has commanded His covenant forever:
Holy and awesome is His name.
The fear of the Lord is the beginning of wisdom;
A good understanding have all those who do His commandments.
His praise endures forever.

Psalm 111

displays both His justice and His mercy on the cross. His justice is seen in Jesus' becoming a curse for us on the cross. He was cut off from all blessedness. He was forsaken. The fury of divine wrath fell upon Him. His pain far exceeded that of thorns and nails because He bore the full torment of the damned. It was the moment of curse.

The unspeakable mercy of God is seen at the same moment in that the curse was directed at our Savior instead of at us. We receive the blessing Christ achieved for His perfect obedience to the Law. In this marvelous transaction, God's justice was preserved in the midst of the triumph of His grace.

If God did not punish sin, He would not be just. If He were not just, He would not be God. Though at times we are terrified at the thought of God's justice, ultimately we take great comfort in it. To know that God is just is to know that ultimately God will make all things right. No injustice will linger for eternity. The just God's plan for His created universe is righteousness. He redeems us for righteousness, by righteousness, and into righteousness.

The Invincible Power

"Could God build a rock so big that He could not move it?"

Seminary professors have been asked this question countless times. The question usually follows a prior question that appears innocent enough: "Professor, is God omnipotent?"

If the unsuspecting teacher answers yes, then comes the question of the rock, posed with a diabolical smile on the student's face.

The professor's dilemma is clear. If he responds yes, he is immediately guilty of declaring that there is something God cannot do—that is, not move the rock. If the professor answers no, he is equally guilty of declaring that God cannot do anything He pleases and there are limits to His power. And the poor professor appears to be a heretic for denying the omnipotence of God.

Some professors handle this question by clever, evasive methods. They reply, "The question is an improper question because it is stated as a complex question." A complex question is one that has internal logic problems of the "Have you stopped beating your wife?" variety. No matter how you answer such a question you condemn yourself.

A complex question is a heads-I-lose, tails-you-win proposition. However, the "God-and-rock" question is not a complex question. The way it is stated is legitimate. Not only is the question properly asked, there is a proper and correct answer, and it affirms the omnipotence of God. The answer is "No, God cannot build a rock so big that He cannot move it."

How can that be? Is there something God cannot do? To understand this answer we must first establish some foundations. First, it is important to note that the word *omnipotent* is an abstract theological term used by theologians in theological conversation. Most theologians do not use the term *omnipotence* in an absolute sense, which would mean that God could do anything, absolutely anything. God could die. God could lie. God could create a square circle. God could be God and not be God at the same time and in the same relationship. Here the concept of omnipotence is pushed to the level of absurdity.

The normal meaning of *omnipotence* is that God has absolute power over His creation. He rules His creation; the creation does not rule Him. God has the entire universe under His control. There are no horses that run too fast for Him to catch them, no elephants too heavy for Him to lift, and no rocks too big for Him to move.

Thus, the answer to the student's question is God cannot build a rock too big for Him to move because God cannot stop being God. He cannot stop acting consistently with His nature. It is His nature to be omnipotent over what He creates.

Someone will surely protest and say, "But cannot God limit His power if He so desires?" Yes, if God desired to limit His power, He could do that. If God decided to sin, He certainly would have the power to carry out His decision. However, would God ever choose to sin or to limit his power? Would God ever choose to subordinate Himself to His own creation? To do so He would have to give up His throne, to stop being God. These questions are at best hypothetical, and if we ask them with full knowledge of all that God is, their inherent absurdity is soon apparent.

We must be careful not to load onto the word *omnipotent* more baggage than it can carry. The word the Bible uses that resembles *omnipotent* is *almighty*. "'I am the Alpha and the Omega, the Beginning and the End,' says the Lord, 'Who is and who was and who is to come, the Almighty'" (Rev. 1:8).

Interestingly God refers to Himself as "the Almighty" in this passage that mentions "the Beginning and the End." The thread of the mighty acts of God is woven throughout Scripture. The Bible reveals His power in creation and His power over creation. We see God's power in redemption and over redemption. From creation to the consummation of God's kingdom, we are brought into contact with One who is Almighty, omnipotent.

I sat in terrified silence the first day of my freshman class in astronomy. The professor posed a question for us: "Suppose that we have a scale wherein an inch equals a million miles. How far would it be to the nearest star apart from our sun? Would it be one hundred feet? three hundred feet? or five hundred feet?"

My mind began to calculate frantically. Twelve inches make one foot. One foot then would mean twelve million miles. Multiply that by one hundred and the first option meant a distance of over a billion miles.

Now, I knew that our sun was ninety-three million miles from the earth. It seemed reasonable that the next nearest star would not be much more than ten times that distance, so I guessed one hundred feet was the correct answer.

I was wrong. So were all the other students who guessed either three hundred feet or five hundred feet. The professor fooled us. He said, "None of the above."

He went on to explain that the nearest star was approximately the distance from Pittsburgh to Chicago with each inch equaling a million miles. He gave us a little more help.

"Light travels at a rate of 186,000 miles per second. That is, in one second light can travel seven-and-a-half times around the earth. The light that we see twinkling at night from the nearest star left that star on its way to Earth four-and-a-half years ago!"

The distance from earth to the nearest star is four-and-a-half light years away. Traveling at a speed of 186,000 miles per second it takes over four years to reach us! I could not fathom such immensity.

When I left that class, I was in a daze. I had mixed feelings. On the one hand, I was staggered by the apparent insignificance of planet Earth and of R. C. Sproul. I felt like a speck in a vast universe. Yet, I was also awestruck by the sheer magnitude of power that could make a universe so gigantic as to contain billions of stars in megabillions of distances from each other.

My mind snapped back to Genesis 1.

God's Power in Creation

Here is the biblical description of God's mighty work of creation:

> In the beginning God created the heavens and the earth. The earth was without form, and void; and darkness was on the face of the deep. And the Spirit of God was hovering over the face of the waters. Then God said, "Let there be light"; and there was light.
> *(Gen. 1:1–3)*

The last line—"and there was light"—is totally mystifying! God spoke. He commanded light to come into existence. Light began to shine. This is what Saint Augustine called the Divine Imperative. The world was created by the sheer power of God's voice.

No artist can speak to his paint and create the Mona Lisa. A sculptor would be called a lunatic for standing in front of a mountain and commanding it to turn into Mount Rushmore. Human beings cannot change the course of nature or bring things into existence by sheer talk. But God can. His voice is almighty.

One of the more puzzling mysteries in the Bible is the power of God in creation. As we saw earlier, only God has the power of being within Himself. In the same way, only God has the absolute power to create.

We use the term *creativity* to describe the skills of human beings. There are creative inventors, creative problem-solvers, creative artists, and so on. But just how creative are creative people? No human artist or inventor brings something into being from nothing. The artist has a medium through which an artistic creation is shaped or arranged. An inventor stands before a workbench and with tools and raw materials "creates" some new gizmo. But no artist or inventor can create a work of art or an invention by the power of his voice.

When we speak of God's power in creation, we speak of His ability to create the world *ex nihilo*, simply meaning "out of nothing." To see the radical character of this idea let us look at an ancient analogy provided by the philosopher Aristotle.

Aristotle was perplexed by the mysteries of change and motion. As he observed changes taking place around him, he noticed different factors involved in the change process. To illustrate these influences, which he called causes, Aristotle used the example of a sculptor creating a statue out of a piece of stone. Aristotle listed the following causes.

1. *The material cause:* What is something made of? In the case of the statue, it is a block of stone.

2. *The instrumental cause:* The tools that are used to bring about change. In the case of the statue, it is the chisel.

3. *The formal cause:* The plan or the blueprint for the change. In the case of the statue, it would be the artist's sketch.

4. *The final cause:* The purpose for the change. In the case of the statue, it would be to make a beautiful object of art.

All of these causes are involved in change, but none of them individually—or all of them together—can bring about the desired change. Something else is required. Aristotle added the *efficient cause* and the *sufficient cause.* An efficient cause is that which is necessary to do the job. A sufficient cause is that which is clearly able to do the job. The two might be the same. In the case of the statue, the sculptor is both the efficient and the sufficient cause. Without the sculptor, there can be no statue.

The sculptor needs tools and materials to do the job. He is efficient and sufficient not in himself but only with the aid of the other elements.

The sixty-four-thousand-dollar question is this: If it is true of men that nothing can come out of nothing, why is it not also true of God? Why is God the grand exception to the rule? If all the power of nature cannot bring something out of nothing how can God do it?

I don't know. I don't have any idea how He does it, and I am completely baffled by God's power to bring something out of nothing. I know that He does it, but I don't know how He does it. I also know that reason demands that we accept the premise that something, somewhere has the ability to create out of nothing or nothing would exist. I also know that reason shows that it is impossible for something to create itself. We have to have a creator. That creator must be eternal. That creator must have the power to create or I would not, indeed I could not, be trying to write about this perplexing issue.

We must also understand the radical difference between saying that the world created itself or in saying that God created the world. An analogy of a magician will help. A magician can make a rabbit appear out of a hat. But do we believe for an instant that the magician creates the rabbit out of nothing? No, we are confident that the magician has gone to great lengths to convince us first that the hat is empty. A mirror down the middle of a half-full hat does have the tendency to convince us that the hat is totally empty. The magician, using a rabbit, a hat, a wand, and a stage creates an illusion. The magician does not create a rabbit.

Now suppose we offer the idea that the universe created itself out of nothing. Suppose that once there was nothing and then—*poof*—suddenly there was something. What caused it? There is no material cause, no instrumental cause, no formal cause, no final cause, and above all no efficient cause or sufficient cause. This act of creation was sheer magic—magic without a magician, without a hat, without a rabbit, without a wand, and without a stage. Something has come from absolutely nothing.

This idea accepts the irrational idea of self-creation, which is a logical absurdity. For something to create itself, it must exist before it is. It must be and not be at the same time. Not even God can do that. Some have called this spontaneous generation, which is a sophisticated synonym for the word *poof*.

Recently, a Nobel-prize-winning physicist wrote an incredible essay. (I will not mention his name to protect the guilty.) In the essay the physicist declared that the time had come for scientists to abandon once and for all the concept of spontaneous generation. He said that spontaneous generation was an impossibility and scientists should no longer appeal to it. So far, so good. Then, to my utter disbelief, this previously credible scholar proposed that now we must speak of gradual spontaneous generation.

Gradual spontaneous generation? Think about it—if you can. The scientist was arguing that something cannot come from nothing quickly. Here the impossible takes a little longer. I get a little mixed up thinking about something that is gradually spontaneous. Or is it spontaneously gradual? My brain must think quickly slowly in order to understand this.

Someone may ask, "Why do we need a creator at all? Why can't we just say that the world itself is eternal? Who needs a creator? Why can't matter be its own explanation?" Without getting into the philosophical problems, here is the shorthand answer: Matter is not sufficient to the task because we see matter change. It changes in appearance, size, shape, weight, age, and in a host of other ways. If we want an explanation for the ultimate cause of change or motion in the world, we must find something that has the power of being in itself. If it lives in the universe, it is still different from the universe because it alone has that unique power of being.

John Gerstner was once asked the question why matter couldn't be the ultimate cause of the universe. He replied, "What's the matter with matter? The matter with matter is that matter has a *mater*."

But have we solved our excruciating problem, how does God create something from nothing? I have poked fun at those who have stumbled and stuttered trying to explain some kind of self-creation out of nothing, but I, too, am still living in a glass house. Is there even a clue to the answer?

When Christians assert that God created the world out of nothing, they do not mean that there was absolutely nothing. God was there. God is eternal. God does not have a beginning. God does not create Himself either spontaneously or gradually. God would be no more able to create Himself than a stone could create itself. What we mean when we say that God created the world out of nothing is that there was no pre-existent matter out of which He shaped the world. There was no *material cause* to the world.

The Christian says that in creation there was an instrumental cause (the Word of God), a formal cause (the plan of God), a final cause (the will of God), and a self-existent Being who is the efficient and sufficient cause. Here, all that is missing is the material cause. For the sculptor that would be fatal. It is not for God.

To put it another way, in the Christian view of Creation, there is no stage, no wand, no hat, and no concealed rabbit. But at least a magician is present. The "magician" happens to be self-existent and eternal. He is omnipotent. I know that He does nothing that is irrational but much that is mysterious. I still don't know how He produced the "rabbit." But I do know that He did it all without mirrors.

God's Power in Miracles

A further glimpse of God's power comes in the Lazarus episode.

> Then Jesus, again groaning in Himself, came to the tomb. It was a cave, and a stone lay against it. Jesus said, "Take away the stone." Martha, the sister of him who was dead, said to Him, "Lord, by this time there is a stench, for he has been dead four days."
>
> Jesus said to her, "Did I not say to you that if you would believe you would see the glory of God?"
>
> Then they took away the stone from the place where the dead man was lying. And Jesus lifted up His eyes and said, "Father, I thank You that You have heard Me. And I know that You always hear Me, but because of the people who are standing by I said this, that they may believe that You sent Me."
>
> Now when He had said these things, He cried with a loud voice, "Lazarus, come forth!"
>
> And he who had died came out bound hand and foot with graveclothes, and his face was wrapped with a cloth. Jesus said to them, "Loose him and let him go." *(John 11:38–44)*

There is a type of familiarity that breeds complacency. The life of Jesus is such a blaze of miracles that we might read a story like that of Lazarus with no sense of astonishment. But think about it—what happened there in Bethany is flat out amazing!

I have seen television preachers lay their hands upon the heads of the sick and cry "Heal!" But I have never seen a preacher go to a cemetery and begin shouting for rotting corpses to burst from their graves. Perhaps some preachers have tried it, but I am sure none have succeeded. (I know that some readers will write and tell me about real, modern resurrections. But none will give evidence of the resurrection of a person who had been dead for four days.)

Jesus did not touch Lazarus. There was no laying on of hands, no mouth-to-mouth resuscitation. Jesus did not administer

CPR. The only preparation for the miracle was the rolling away of the stone. Then Jesus yelled to Lazarus. How strange. But the most bizarre part of the story is that it worked. The putrid flesh of Lazarus was instantly healed. Air filled his lungs. His heart began to pulsate. The veins in his temples throbbed. He was alive. He quit his grave.

That is power. That is almighty power. That is the same kind of power by which God created the world.

God's Power in Redemption

The same power God displayed in the Creation and in His miracles is also exhibited in His plan of redemption. The God who set the heavens in motion is the God who set Pharaoh on his ear. He heard the groans of His people in bondage and delivered them through the Exodus from Egypt.

Throughout this experience of the Jewish people, God manifested His mighty power. From the plagues that struck Egypt to the manna dropped from heaven in the wilderness, the power of God was on display. The power of Moses faltered; the power of the people was suspect. But God's power endured.

After the miraculous provision of manna from heaven, the people of Israel began to complain and grumble. They were sick and tired of manna. They had manna for breakfast, manna for lunch, manna for dinner, and if they wanted a midnight snack, they had but one option—manna. They cursed their bad luck and spoke with nostalgia about the good old days in Egypt. They yearned to return to their slavery where they at least had enjoyed the taste of leeks, garlics, cucumbers, and onions (see Num. 11:4–6).

When the people whined to Moses, he took his case to God, asking to be relieved of his command. Moses was staggering under the burden of leading such a rebellious crowd: "I am not able to bear all these people alone, because the burden is too heavy for me. If you treat me like this, please kill me here and now—if I have found favor in Your sight—and do not let me see my wretchedness!" (Num. 11:14–15).

God's response showed anger mixed with a kind of humorous irony. He promised to deliver exactly what the people were begging for. They wanted meat to eat? Meat they would get—more meat than they ever dreamed of:

> " 'Therefore the LORD will give you meat, and you shall eat. You shall eat, not one day, nor two days, nor five days, nor ten days, nor twenty days, but for a whole month, until it comes out of your nostrils and becomes loathsome to you, because you have despised the LORD who is among you, and have wept before Him, saying, "Why did we ever come up out of Egypt?" ' "
> *(Num. 11:18b–20)*

Now it was Moses' turn to stumble in unbelief. He had witnessed the power of God at Sinai. He had watched the waters part at the Red Sea. He had seen the explosive power of God in action countless times, but now he faltered. Had God gone too far this time? Was God making threats He couldn't possibly back up with real power.

> And Moses said, "The people whom I am among are six hundred thousand men on foot; yet You have said, 'I will give them meat, that they may eat for a whole month.' Shall flocks and herds be slaughtered for them, to provide enough for them? Or shall all the fish of the sea be gathered together for them, to provide enough for them?"
> *(Num. 11:21–22)*

Moses was clearly challenging the omnipotence of God. He did not see the full range of divine possibility. He staggered at the enormity of the task of feeding so many people for such a long time. The scope of the miracle would far exceed what Jesus would do centuries later in feeding the five thousand. Jesus fed five thousand for one lunch; the Father was about to feed more than six hundred thousand for an entire month.

Moses raised his doubts. He was certain the task was too great, even for God. God responded: "And the LORD said to Moses, 'Has the LORD's arm been shortened? Now you shall see whether My word will befall you or not' " (Num. 11:23).

When the Scripture speaks of God's power, a frequent image used is the "right arm." Moses had seen the Lord's strong right arm in action. God asked Moses if that arm had suddenly become crippled. God's arm does not wither. His muscles do not atrophy with the passing of the ages.

The strength of men, though, is but for a season. No one reigns as the heavyweight champion forever. Even the muscles of Muhammad Ali have turned to flab. Age and now disease have robbed him of his former strength. That is the way with men. It is not the way with God. There is no increase nor decline to His strength. His omnipotence is immutable, eternal, infinite. His right arm does not grow short.

The right arm of the Lord brought the people out of Egypt and fed them in their hunger. The task of redemption is not assigned to God's left hand. All of His divine strength is given to the task. The same power stands behind the gospel, a power that Paul said was "unto salvation" (Rom. 1:16).

The peasant girl Mary understood the power of God's right hand, although it took her a while to grasp the full import of what was happening to her. At first she, like Moses, faltered at the message of God. When Gabriel announced she was going to have a baby, Mary said, "How can that be, since I do not know a man?"

> And the angel answered and said to her, "The Holy Spirit will come upon you, and the power of the Highest will over- shadow you; therefore, also, that Holy One who is to be born will be called the Son of God. Now indeed, Elizabeth your relative has also conceived a son in her old age; and this is now the sixth month for her who was called barren. For with God nothing will be impossible." *(Luke 1:35–37)*

With God nothing will be impossible. In one sense this is an overstatement, an example of biblical hyperbole. There are things, as we have seen, that are impossible for God. God cannot lie; He cannot die. Here the angel speaks a sound theological statement, fully understanding that God's power and possibilities are in relationship to His sovereignty over His creation. But if the ordinary means by which a baby is born are not what God desires in this case, He has the power to use extraordinary means.

Mary assumed the impossibility of such an event and is registered as the first skeptic of the virgin birth. The second skeptic was Joseph. Mary assumed that because a virgin birth would be irregular it would be impossible. She made the mistake of thinking that because God has ordered certain things to occur in certain ways many times, He is therefore bound always and everywhere to that same pattern.

The angel listened patiently to Mary's skepticism but then reminded her, "With God all things are possible." The virgin birth was not a subject of skepticism for Gabriel. He was well versed in the power of God. His angelic duty placed him in the presence of God in the heavenly court every day. He had no reason to doubt the power of God.

In short order Mary became a believer. Her response to the angel indicated her spirit: "Behold the maidservant of the Lord! Let it be to me according to your word" (Luke 1:38). This response of the mother of God may be the most profound confession of faith ever recorded in Scripture. Here she declared her total willingness to submit to the authority and the power of God. "Let it be to me"—this is to say, "Do what you will to me, God."

For most of us, if there is a place where we want to limit the omnipotence of God, it is in respect to what He does to *us*. Prayer for us is often a kind of room service menu, and we call in our orders to the heavenly bellhop. Prayer becomes the means by which we tell God what He needs to do for us. Prayer is our power to control His power.

Mary did not allow her concept of God to degenerate to such a level. She knew who God was and she knew who Mary was. He was Lord; she was servant. Her will was to submit to God's will. God gives the orders. Gabriel did not come to Mary to request a virgin birth or to negotiate the plan of redemption. Gabriel came with an announcement. That is why this portion of Scripture is called the "Annunciation." No one calls it the "Negotiation."

Shortly after the Annunciation, Mary went to visit her cousin, Elizabeth. There, inspired by the Holy Spirit, Mary sang the Magnificat, "My soul doth magnify the Lord":

"For He who is mighty has done great things for me,
And holy is His name.
And His mercy is on those who fear Him
From generation to generation.
He has shown strength with His arm;
He has scattered the proud in the imagination of their hearts.
He has put down the mighty from their thrones,

And exalted the lowly."   *(Luke 1:49–52, italics mine)*

The irony of Mary's song is that she sang of One who used His strength to help her after she declared "Do whatever you wish with me." She combined her understanding of God's omnipotence with her understanding of God's mercy and grace. In redemption God's power is gracious power. The greatest song we can ever sing is, "For He who is mighty has done great things for me."

That God has used His power "for us" is what redemption is all about. For the unbeliever, the idea of God's omnipotence provokes sheer terror. For those who embrace the gospel, God's omnipotence brings sweet comfort. The One who has all power loves us and calls us His children.

We all are aware of our weakness and vulnerability. Even as children we called upon the superior power of others to come to our aid. The childish boast "My father can whip your father" reveals a deeply rooted desire to have ultimate power on our side. That is the power that God has put on the side of the redeemed. That power backs up His divine claims and promises.

The Authority of Jesus

When Jesus was on earth He displayed remarkable powers. He raised Lazarus from the dead and performed many other miracles. His contemporaries noted an element of His power that we sometimes do not—the power of His speaking. The gospel writers reported that Jesus did not speak like the scribes and the Pharisees but as one "having authority" (see Matt. 7:29).

The Greek word *exousia*, used in the New Testament to describe Jesus' authority, is translated in English as "authority" and at other times as "power." The English words can be combined to make "powerful authority" or "authoritative power." The Greek word itself is a compound word, its roots literally meaning "out of being" or "out of substance."

The Greek quest for ultimate reality was a quest for ultimate being or ultimate substance. It is noteworthy that, though the content of the New Testament must be understood in light of its Jewish background and flavor, nevertheless the Holy Spirit found the Greek language an adequate medium by which to convey the word of God recorded in the New Testament. If we push antipathy to Greek culture too far, as some modern Christian scholars wish to do, we may do violence to the scriptural text. Here the use of the word *ousia* as the root word for powerful authority is a case in which we see the utter adequacy of Greek to express a truth of God.

When Jesus spoke as "One having authority," He spoke "out of substance." His words were weighty. They were not thinly disguised smoke screens. His words were not empty. In contrast to the scribes and Pharisees, the teaching of Jesus was full, rich, and powerful.

Behind the authority of Jesus stood the omnipotent power of God, the link to Jesus' *divine* authority. The very word *authority* hints at a connection to the word *authorship*. God is the omnipotent author of His creation. He is the omnipotent redeemer of His creation. He exercises omnipotent authority over His creation.

The Father had given all authority on heaven and on earth to Jesus. With those credentials, it is no wonder that the contemporaries of Jesus referred to Him as One who spoke with authority.

Power for the Future

The omnipotent power of God is not limited to creation and redemption. God has committed the same power into the future. There is a future for the people of God precisely because God's omnipotence will have no end.

The vision the Apostle John received on the Isle of Patmos gives a glimpse of the future power of God.

And I saw a new heaven and a new earth, for the first heaven and the first earth had passed away. Also there was no more sea. Then I, John, saw the holy city, New Jerusalem, coming down out of heaven from God, prepared as a bride adorned for her husband. And I heard a loud voice from heaven saying, "Behold, the tabernacle of God is with men, and He will dwell with them, and they shall be His people, and God Himself will be with them and be their God. *(Rev. 21:1–3)*

The zeal of the Lord of Hosts will perform these things. The One who is altogether omnipotent can carry out every

138

For the word of the Lord is right,
And all His work is done in truth.
He loves righteousness and justice;
The earth is full of the goodness of the Lord.
By the word of the Lord the heavens were made,
And all the host of them by the breath of His mouth.
He gathers the waters of the sea together as a heap;
He lays up the deep in storehouses.
Let all the earth fear the Lord;
Let all the inhabitants of the world stand in awe of Him.
For He spoke, and it was done;
He commanded, and it stood fast.
The Lord brings the counsel of the nations to nothing;
He makes the plans of the peoples of no effect.
The counsel of the Lord stands forever,
The plans of His heart to all generations.
Blessed is the nation whose God is the Lord,
And the people whom He has chosen as His own inheritance.

Psalm 33:4–12

promise He has made. That power is immutably wed to His divine integrity. Therefore, there is a guaranteed future for the people of God.

This is the crux of the matter: God is able to do what He says He will do. He has the power to raise our bodies from the dust. He has the power to wipe away our tears forever. He has the power to cleanse us from all sin. His promises are not idle wishes. They are commitments.

When I make a commitment for the future, there is always a tacit assumption connected to it. If I agree to speak somewhere three years from now, it is assumed that I will keep the promise *if I am able*. I may be dead in three years. I may be physically incapacitated. I may be hindered in some other way.

There is no "if" with God's future promises. He will do what He has promised.

Can I Trust You, God?

Jesus was on trial, His life in the hands of a second-rate Roman procurator. In the formal interrogation of his prisoner, Pontius Pilate addressed some urgent questions to Jesus. One of them concerned Jesus' political aspirations. The Jews had brought Jesus to Pilate charging that Jesus had claimed to be King of the Jews. Pilate pressed the question:

Pilate therefore said to Him, "Are You a king then?" Jesus answered, "You say rightly that I am a king. For this cause I was born, and for this cause I have come into the world, that I should bear witness to the truth. Everyone who is of the truth hears My voice." Pilate said to Him, "What is truth?"

(John 18:37–38)

What is truth? I have often wondered how Pilate asked this question. What was his tone of voice? What kind of expression did he have on his face? Was the question raised in jest? Was it cynical? Was Pilate pensive for a moment? We don't really know. If Pilate was momentarily concerned for truth, his mood soon gave way to a spirit of expediency. If he cared about knowing the truth, he certainly didn't care much about doing the truth. Immediately after asking Jesus the question, he went out to the Jews and reported, "I find no fault in Him at all" (John 18:38). Here he did speak the unvarnished truth. He couldn't find fault in Jesus because there wasn't any fault there to find. No one could find fault. Neither Pilate nor any investigator could have found what was not there.

People could accuse Jesus of faults. People could invent or imagine faults in Jesus. But to find real fault in Jesus was an impossible task. He was the only sane human being ever to dare to ask his enemies, "Which of you convicts Me of sin?" (John 8:46) without fear of being embarrassed.

To declare that Jesus was without fault and then minutes later to turn Him over to a barbarous mob was to slaughter the truth. Pilate judged the Truth. He sentenced the Truth. He scourged the Truth. He mocked the Truth. He crucified the Truth.

The irony is that at the very moment he asked his question "What is truth?" he was staring at the pure incarnation of Truth. The One who is the Truth had just said to him, "Everyone who is of the truth hears My voice."

Pilate missed that voice. The words bounced off his ears. He was not "of the truth."

What is truth? In his later years Francis Schaeffer frequently spoke of "true truth." What a strange expression. The phrase "true truth" is such an obvious redundancy we wonder why anyone would be tempted to speak in this manner. It is like speaking of a circular circle or a squarish square or a beautiful beauty.

Francis Schaeffer didn't stutter. He had a powerful reason to speak of true truth, and he used this terminology to distinguish what he was talking about from other popular notions of truth in our culture. True truth refers to objective truth. It is a kind of truth that is not slippery. It sticks. It has staying power.

When I was a boy a popular song hit the top of the charts in Tin Pan Alley. The title was puzzling to me: "You're as Hard to Hold as Quicksilver." I got the gist of the lyrics, but I didn't know what quicksilver was. Soon I discovered that mercury was sometimes called quicksilver because it looks like liquid silver and is almost impossible to hang on to.

Modern views of truth tend to be as hard to hold as quicksilver. They slip through our fingers. It has become fashionable to speak of truth as something that is relative. The reference point for relative truth is the individual. The idea goes like this: "Something is true for me if I think it is true or if I find it meaningful."

My favorite illustration of this view comes from a discussion I once had with a college student. We had been discussing the existence of God, and during our conversation the student said to me, "If believing in God makes you feel good, then for you there is a God. But I don't feel the need for religion. For me there is no God."

This was a living, breathing example of relative truth. I became frustrated with this student because I found it difficult to find common ground for communication. Finally, I said, "But I am talking about a God who exists apart from me and apart from you. I am talking about a God who exists whether we believe in Him or not!"

The student seemed to grow more thoughtful. Was I breaking through? I went on, "If God does not exist objectively, according to true truth, then all my prayers, all my devotion, all my religious fervor cannot bring Him into existence. I have the power to imagine things that are not really there, but I cannot ultimately create such things out of nothing. By the same token if such a God does in fact exist then all of your unbelief does not have the power to destroy Him. The God of whom I am speaking does not pass in and out of existence at our whims."

Suddenly the discussion moved to a different plane. We moved to a discussion of a God who is real.

To speak of truth in utterly relativistic terms is to have a mindless view of truth. Truth is then defined by feelings or emotions or some other reference point, but it cannot involve much thinking. In order to grasp truth with the mind, one must think. The thoughts we have cannot be arbitrary or chaotic if we want to understand truth. Relativistic thinking is quicksilver thinking.

When we speak of true truth or objective truth we are talking about what philosophers call real states of affairs. *Real states of affairs* is merely a fancy way of describing reality. Howard Cosell made the saying popular, "Tell it like it is!" Cosell was asking for reality. He didn't want opinions or emotions; he wanted objective reality.

When Cosell spoke about controversial matters, Cosell often defended the statements others found outrageous by saying, "I am only telling it like it is." His opponents would counter that Cosell was "telling it like it is" as Cosell saw it. That is the problem; can we ever be sure that "the way it is" is really the way it is? How much personal bias and prejudice do we bring to every situation? If there is such a thing as real states of affairs, can we ever escape our own subjectivity enough to know them?

We know the power of prejudice. The power to distort reality is a force we carry around with us. But no matter how deep our prejudice, it does not destroy the fact that reality exists. Reality exists apart from us and is not dependent upon us.

Who then defines and knows reality? Is there anyone who has the ability always and everywhere to "tell it like it is"? Such a person must be sure that he understands reality from every conceivable angle and vantage point. He must be without prejudice and error.

God, of course, has a perfect understanding of reality. His grasp of real states of affairs is perfect. He is the fountain of all truth, the embodiment of all truth, and the perceiver of all truth. In Him are no falsehoods, no distortions, no errors. He tells it like it is.

The best definition for truth may be this: *Truth is reality as it is perceived by God.* In this definition there is no slipping and sliding into relativity. Here truth is true, because God's perception of truth is perfect.

The Jewish View of Truth

For the Old Testament Jew, truth was a sacred matter. Truth involved a proper understanding of reality, but it also involved much more than that. For the Jew truth also had a personal dimension, an emotional dimension, and an ethical dimension.

Truth is personal—it is a special part of any close human relationship. Trust is a by-product of truth, and personal relationships are built upon trust. I trust people who demonstrate that they are truthful. I do not trust people who show themselves to be habitual liars. A person who is trustworthy is a person who is truthful.

Broken truth hurts. Satan, "the father of lies," loves to attack and distort truth. The Scripture says that Satan was a liar from the beginning. It is painful for anybody to invest his heart in a lie. A broken truth often means a broken heart.

This is the problem with lies. We do invest our hearts in the promises people make and the stories they tell us. When the promises are not kept and the stories prove to be false, we are hurt. We are disillusioned. We sometimes grow bitter. Trust is a fragile commodity and is as precious as it is delicate. Deep levels of trust take years to develop. Yet, such trust can be smashed to pieces in seconds.

Every time we experience a broken trust we find it harder to trust again. The cynical person is often a bitter person. His cynicism is a result of and an expression of his pain. We have an expression, "Fool me once, shame on you. Fool me twice, shame on me." Every time a lie is exposed we are more reluctant to believe anyone's claim to truth.

Honesty is a virtue that is exalted even among pagans, who sometimes make statements like this: "I may cheat on my wife but at least I'm honest about it." Obviously, this is distorted thinking. To cheat on your wife is to violate truth and to break a promise. But when a person says, "At least I'm honest about it," attention is called to some virtue left in the misdeed. At least what society considers the worse crime—hypocrisy— has not been committed. Hypocrisy is a special form of the lie, involving fraud. The hypocrite is a play-actor pretending to be something he's not. The hypocrite does not merely tell lies with his mouth; he lies with his life.

Jesus reserved the sharpest personal criticism for the Pharisees. He charged them with being hypocrites. Here Jesus reflected the societal revulsion for the hypocrite. Jesus understood that hypocrisy is devastating to those who practice it and to those who are injured by it. The hypocrite cheapens truth and destroys trust.

Every one of us has been fooled and fooled badly in our lives. We know the experience of shattered hopes and broken promises. The sad part is that we, too, have been perpetrators of untruth. We have played the role of the hypocrite.

A pastor is particularly vulnerable to hypocrisy. We are called to be models of righteousness and proclaimers of the truth, but I have never met a preacher whose life was as pure as the gospel he preached. Going in to the job, we know we can never be worthy of the calling or equal to the task. There is a heavy temptation to pretend we have matured spiritually more than we have, and people expect us to be more righteous than we are. Not wanting to let them down, we seek to conceal our weaknesses. Preachers tend to have larger closets than other folks. This is partly because Christians demand that their pastors' skeletons be carefully hidden.

Obviously, it is not good for preachers or anyone else to flaunt their weaknesses before the world. The point is that those who are Christian leaders, those who are models, are especially vulnerable to the temptation of pretense.

Lies beget lies. When we tell or act a lie and someone believes us, we have to buoy it up with more lies to keep it afloat. If someone threatens to reveal the lie, we work to cover it up. All of this works together to undermine the fragile virtue of truth.

So much lying goes on that we may wonder, *Is there anyone we can trust?* We know that it is important to trust God, but we also need someone with skin on whom we can trust. Being trustworthy is linked to our understanding of truth. It is the personal element of truth.

It is one thing for us to know facts; it is another to keep our promises. Albert Einstein once shocked a student when he confessed that he didn't know how many feet there were in a mile. The student could not fathom that the world's greatest mathematical genius could be ignorant of a fact that every schoolboy knows. Einstein explained to the incredulous student that he made it a practice not to clutter his mind with information that he could easily find in a book.

Einstein understood how easy it is to amass facts. It is quite another feat to amass trust. Trust is built by laying a foundation upon truth. It requires more than simply storing up facts. It means observing behavioral patterns—that is, trust comes more from what we do than from what we know.

Trust involves relying less on what we see than upon what we hear. In the New Testament we are told that we walk by faith and not by sight. This faith is what the Bible says comes by "hearing, and hearing by the word of God" (Rom. 10:17). What we hear from God must not be confused with hearsay or with rumor. What God says can be trusted because He only speaks the truth. The Christian walks by faith because he has discovered that God can be trusted.

The biblical word *amen* comes from the ancient Semitic word for truth. When the Jewish congregation heard something that struck a responsive chord, they said amen. That practice has survived, and the "Amen corner" still thrives in some churches. When the people say amen, they mean "That is true."

Jesus made an unusual use of the Jewish word *amen*. Instead of waiting for the amen as a response to what He taught, He used it to begin His teaching. Frequently, He said, "Amen, Amen, I say to you." Our Bibles translate this, "Truly, truly, I say unto you."

Jesus not only says amen, He is *the* Amen. He is called the Amen because of His utter trustworthiness. He is the One who is faithful. Here faithfulness is a synonym for trustworthiness, and these virtues are the very essence of Christianity. The Christian life, which is based on trust, must reflect and mirror truth.

Doing the Truth

For the Jew, truth was more than a noun. In addition to hearing and speaking the truth, the Jew was concerned about doing the truth or living according to truth. Above all it meant keeping his word.

In the New Testament Jesus warned about the taking of vows:

> "Again you have heard that it was said to those of old, 'You shall not swear falsely, but shall perform your oaths to the Lord.' But I say to you, do not swear at all: neither by heaven, for it is God's throne; nor by the earth, for it is His footstool; nor by Jerusalem, for it is the city of the great King. Nor shall you swear by your head, because you cannot make one hair white or black. But let your 'Yes' be 'Yes,' and your 'No,' 'No.' For whatever is more than these is from the evil one."
>
> *(Matt. 5:33–37)*

The meaning of this is difficult to understand. It seems to say it is wrong for Christians ever to take vows or oaths.

Because of these words, some Christians refuse to swear on the Bible in law courts. But is Jesus absolutely prohibiting the taking of vows? Does His teaching here mean that marriage vows, for example, ought not to be taken?

The answer is partly revealed in that vows and oaths are mentioned in the New Testament after Jesus preached this sermon. The Apostle Paul, for example, uttered an oath even while he was writing under the inspiration of the Holy Spirit.

> I tell the truth in Christ, I am not lying, my conscience also bearing me witness in the Holy Spirit, that I have great sorrow and continual grief in my heart. For I could wish myself were accursed from Christ for my brethren, my kinsmen according to the flesh. *(Rom. 9:1–3)*

Here Paul swore an oath by the Holy Spirit. By doing this he was consistent with the biblical pattern of oath-taking. In the Old Testament the vow was established as a sacred promise made to God. As such a promise the vow was an act of worship. The oath was a promise made between men with God as a witness.

To swear by God was a sober and serious matter for the Old Testament Jew, and the practice was reserved for very special occasions. It was considered idolatry to make light of oath-swearing by saying things like, "Cross my heart, hope to die, stick a needle in my eye." The oath was a sacred promise, binding the person who swore the oath.

In the Sermon on the Mount Jesus spoke out against people swearing by all sorts of things other than God Himself. They would swear by the altar or by the throne of God. They swore by things that were near to the sacred and Holy One, but not by the Holy One Himself. Jesus severely rebuked this practice among the Jews. Why? First, such oath-taking involved a kind of fudging. Instead of swearing by God Himself and calling upon God as the witness, people swore upon the altar. The altar had no eyes or ears. The altar was not omniscient nor omnipresent. The altar would never act as the Supreme Judge. To swear by the altar was like making a promise with our fingers crossed. It allowed an escape hatch.

Second, Jesus prohibited this kind of oath-taking because it was idolatrous. Here is how the Jewish reasoning proceeded:

An appeal to God in oath-taking was an act of worship. To appeal to anything less than God was to worship something that was less than God. To worship something that was less than God was idolatry.

Behind this very sober approach to oath-taking stands the holy law of God. In the Ten Commandments we find two commandments that bear directly on oaths and vows. The third commandment reads: "You shall not take the name of the LORD your God in vain, for the LORD will not hold him guiltless who takes His name in vain" (Exod. 20:7). What is taking the Lord's name in vain? Usually, we think this means uttering profanities. Obviously, profanity and blasphemy involve a vain use of the name of God. However, in the original giving of the Law at Mount Sinai, the primary concern of this commandment was the keeping of oaths. To swear by God's name in a cavalier fashion was to insult the majesty of God.

The other commandment bearing on this matter is the ninth commandment: "You shall not bear false witness against your neighbor" (Exod. 20:16).

Bearing false witness was lying while under a solemn and holy oath—the Jewish equivalent to perjury. It is consistent with biblical law for the state to require an oath before God in a courtroom. To bear false witness under oath is to injure the persons on trial and to desecrate the name of God.

When Jesus said that our answers should be "Yes," "Yes," and "No," "No," He was warning about the seriousness of keeping our word and of the dangers involved with taking solemn vows (see Matt. 5:37). They are to be reserved for weighty occasions.

At the same time, a Christian is one who should not have to take an oath in order to be trusted. He should not have to "put it in writing." His yes should be sufficient to indicate a firm commitment. When we say yes, people act upon that word. An expectation is created. We have an obligation to keep that yes.

But no Christian has so much integrity that his word can be trusted absolutely. That is why sacred vows and oaths are necessary. For me to trust that you will be at a meeting on time does not require that you sign a contract or take a sacred oath. But for my wife to trust my intentions in marriage, she needed more than a simple, "Sure, I'll be faithful." She wanted a vow, an oath sworn before God. She wanted a formal covenant before she was willing to trust herself body and soul to the likes of me.

If men were not sinful, then oaths and vows would never be necessary. A simple yes would do. But we are sinful. Nobody's word is absolutely good. Sometimes people get insulted when we ask them for something more than their word. My pride is injured when I have to produce all sorts of identification in a store before my check is accepted.

People demand more than our naked word because they have been hurt in the past by people whose word was not good. This is not a problem foisted upon us only because of the lack of integrity in others. Let's be honest. All of us have broken our word. We should not be indignant when someone wants more from us than our word.

Christians, though, are required to be models of truth. Our word should be sacred, and we need to cultivate a scrupulous concern for our word. Here is where the depth of true spirituality shows itself. A spiritual person is one whose word you can trust. This Christian has integrity and keeps promises. In so doing, the person bears witness to the truthfulness of the God being worshiped and served.

The God of Covenants

The historical method for bringing human beings into a relationship with the living God is by a covenant. A covenant is a contract, a promissory agreement. There can be no covenant without the swearing of an oath. When Abraham was redeemed, he swore an oath to God. The sign of that oath was the rite of circumcision. The New Testament sign of promise is the sacrament of baptism.

Every time we celebrate the Lord's Supper we are renewing our vows of the New Covenant. When we eat of His body and drink of His blood, we are making a fresh promise of commitment to Him. God takes these vows seriously.

So much of life is built upon covenants. My job is based on a contract. The United States is a nation where the form of government is called a social contract under God between the governors and the governed. Most important of all, however, our salvation is based on a covenant. I am redeemed because of a promise. Without the promise of God I have nothing, I am nothing.

If you were thrown into prison and were permitted to have only one book, which book would you request? Like me you might take the Bible. Taking this one step further, if I could have only one chapter of the Bible, I would select the fifteenth chapter of Genesis. And if I could have only one verse, it would be Genesis 15:17, my favorite verse: "And it came to pass, when the sun went down and it was dark, that behold, there was a smoking oven and a burning torch that passed between those pieces."

These words set my soul on fire. It is the passage I turn to when I am assaulted by doubt for it fuels my hope and restores my faith. At best, my faith is frail and weak. Since my faith comes to me from hearing, and hearing from the Word of God (see Rom. 10:17), this is the word of God that I need to hear over and over again.

When I mention my enraptured feelings about Genesis 15:17, when I rhapsodize over this text, people often look at me as if I have lost my senses. "Why," they ask, "is that verse so important?"

To grasp its full significance we must look at its context. This verse is part of a narrative telling of a meeting between God and Abraham. Abraham and his wife Sarah were childless, yet God had promised them an heir. Abraham had his doubts. It is very difficult to be the father of a great nation if you don't have any children. In the face of Abraham's struggle of faith, God took him outside at night and spoke to him:

> "Look now toward heaven, and count the stars if you are able to number them." And He said to him, "So shall your descendants be." And he believed in the LORD, and He accounted it to him for righteousness. Then He said to him, "I am the LORD, who brought you out of Ur of the Chaldeans, to give you this land to inherit it." (Gen. 15:5–7)

God made a promise to Abraham, and the Bible says that Abraham believed that promise. But he believed it with the kind of faith we all have—weak faith. His faith was like that of the New Testament saint who said, "Lord, I believe; help my unbelief" (Mark 9:24). Abraham vacillated. He responded to God with a plaintive cry: "And he said, 'Lord GOD, how shall I know that I will inherit it?'" (Gen. 15:8).

How shall I know? That was Abraham's question. It is also our question. God's promise stretched Abraham's faith to the breaking point. He wanted more than a simple yes from God. He wanted absolute proof that God would do what He had promised.

God accommodated Abraham. He instructed him to enact an elaborate ritual by which animals were cut asunder.

> So He said to him, "Bring Me a three-year-old heifer, a three-year-old female goat, a three-year-old ram, a turtledove, and a young pigeon."
> Then he brought all these to Him and cut them in two, down the middle, and placed each piece opposite the other; but he did not cut the birds in two. *(Gen. 15:9–10)*

The carving of the animals signified a cutting rite. In the ancient world covenants were not written, they were cut. The very word *covenant* comes from the Hebrew word for "cutting." Abraham followed God's detailed instructions and carved up the animals. What followed was a drama that touches the faith of all believers: "And it came to pass, when the sun went down and it was dark, that behold, there was a smoking oven and a burning torch that passed between those pieces" (Gen. 15:17).

Our attention is fixed upon the smoking oven and the burning torch. The elements of fire and smoke are a part of a dramatic theophany—a visible manifestation of God. God appeared to Moses in a burning bush. He led the children of Israel by a pillar of smoke. He is an "all-consuming fire." The torch that moved between the pieces of the carved animals was God Himself.

The meaning of the drama is clear: As God passed between the pieces His message was, "Abraham, if I fail to keep my promise to you, may I be cut asunder just as those animals have been torn apart." God put His eternal being on the line. It was as if He were saying, "May My immutable deity suffer mutation if I break My promise. May My infinite character

I will sing of the mercies of the Lord forever;
With my mouth will I make known
Your faithfulness to all generations.
For I have said, "Mercy shall be built up forever;
Your faithfulness You shall establish in the very heavens.
I have made a covenant with My chosen,
I have sworn to My servant David:
'Your seed I will establish forever,
And build up your throne to all generations.'"
And the heavens will praise Your wonders, O Lord;
Your faithfulness also in the congregation of the saints.
For who in the heavens can be compared to the Lord?
Who among the sons of the mighty can be likened to the Lord?
God is greatly to be feared in the assembly of the saints,
And to be held in reverence by all those who are around Him.
O Lord God of hosts,
Who is mighty like You, O Lord?
Your faithfulness also surrounds You.

Psalm 89:1–8

become finite, my immortal essence suffer mortality. May the impossible become possible if I lie."

The author of Hebrews centuries later reflected on this event when he wrote, "Because He could swear by no one greater, He swore by Himself" (Heb. 6:13).

The surety of God's promise is God Himself. All that He is stands behind His promise. It would not do for God to swear by the temple or by His mother's grave. He has no mother. The temple is not sacred enough to confirm the oath of God. He must swear by His own integrity, using His divine nature as an everlasting guarantee.

We must not forget that the promise God made was not limited to Abraham; it was made to Abraham and "to [his] descendants after [him—his seed]" (see Gen. 17:7). That means the promise God swore by Himself was sworn to you, to me, and to all who participate by faith in the covenant promise.

We can trust God because He has promised by His own being. It is no more possible for God to lie to us than it is for His eternal being to disintegrate. His passing through the pieces was a divine form of circumcision.

Abraham's circumcision was the human sign and seal of Abraham's promise to God. The covenant had two parties. The agreement was made between God and man. The symbol of circumcision was a nonverbal promise. For Abraham's part the rite signified this: "May I be cut off from you, God, from all your benefits, all your mercy, just as I have cut off the foreskin of my flesh, if I break this covenant."

The rite of circumcision was a sign of Abraham's blessing, a sign of being separated from fallenness unto redemption. On the negative side, circumcision was a symbol of the curse of God. To be cursed by God is to be cut off from His presence and from His benefits.

The children of Abraham broke the covenant. They carried the menacing sign of the curse on their bodies. God broke no promises. He remained a covenant-keeper while we were covenant-breakers.

The ultimate drama of redemption occurred on the Cross. Here the Son of God took upon Himself the curse of Abraham's seed. Jesus underwent the ultimate act of circumcision, not for Himself, but for us.

God kept His promise even when we broke ours. His commitment to the covenant of redemption was greater than ours. He kept the faith. He keeps us in the faith. This is the supreme evidence of His trustworthiness. His word is true. He keeps His promises.

The Love That Will Not Let Us Go

When Karl Barth, the famed German theologian, visited the United States, a student at a seminary supposedly asked, "Dr. Barth, what is the single most important truth you have learned as a theologian?"

Barth replied, "The most important thing I have learned is this: 'Jesus loves me this I know, for the Bible tells me so.'"

"Jesus loves me" is the central affirmation of the Christian faith and sets it apart from any mere abstract philosophy. Christianity has many weighty principles. Christianity has a sober ethic. Yet at the heart of the faith is the commitment to a personal relationship with a personal God.

We have seen that God is infinite, eternal, self-existent, immutable, and a host of other things. These attributes reveal a Creator/Redeemer who is majestic in His transcendent greatness. But imagine all of these attributes collected together in an abstract being who is devoid of feelings and incapable of personal responses.

If God were merely a self-existent, eternal field of energy, who would ever want to worship Him? How could we have fellowship with an impersonal force? People do love impersonal objects, but such relationships tend to grow boring. When I was a teenager, there was a time when I "loved" my car. I waxed the finish and polished the chrome every day. But the only way my car could respond to my affection was to gleam in the sunshine and roar when I ignited the engine. The car could not speak to me nor love me. I gave it a name, but I was not able to make it a person.

The Bible cuts through all the philosophic abstractions and declares that God is a Person. As a personal being God is capable of loving and being loved. The God we worship is the God of Abraham, Isaac, and Jacob. Abraham, Isaac, and Jacob were all people, and that means that God is a God of people. He is a personal God with whom human persons can have a love relationship.

The truth about a personal God is set forth clearly in the New Testament:

> Beloved, let us love one another, for love is of God; and everyone who loves is born of God and knows God. He who does not love does not know God, for God is love. In this the love of God was manifested toward us, that God has sent His only begotten Son into the world, that we might live through Him. In this is love, not that we loved God, but that He loved us and sent His Son to be the propitiation for our sins. Beloved, if God so loved us, we also ought to love one another.
>
> *(1 John 4:7–11)*

"God is love" is the bold assertion of this text. The biblical writer is not content merely to write that God is loving or that God loves. He takes the radical plunge and says that God is love.

How are we to understand this? If God literally is love, does that mean that there is an absolute identity between God and love? If such an identity existed then the words "God is love" would be a tautology. This means the identity between love and God would be so pure that we could reverse the order of the words without changing the meaning—Love is God.

Turning the words of Scripture around in this fashion does serious violence to what the Bible is teaching and should not be done. There can be no love in this world without God. God is the source and fountainhead of all love. Even the love of pagans for each other is a reflection of the ultimate Source of love. Yet we still cannot say that love is God because we experience types of love that are ungodly. Though God is love, He is more than love. To say simply that He is love is to reduce Him to but one of His attributes.

The temptation to reduce God to love alone is strong, especially when we fear His wrath or seek to flee from His justice. If we could strip God of all His attributes except for love, we would have nothing to fear from the Last Judgment. But to separate the love of God from His other attributes is impossible. God will not tolerate it. The love of God is a holy and righteous love. But His love does not compromise His integrity.

I once heard an intriguing lecture on the character of the Apostle Paul. The speaker used the letters of Paul's name to describe four of the apostle's chief characteristics. The last two letters in his name, the *u* and the *l*, stood for the words *uncompromising* and *loving*. The professor stressed that Paul was a man of conviction. He was not blown about with every wind of doctrine. He was bold for the truth. He refused to negotiate the nonnegotiable. He would not tolerate the intolerable. Paul was a man of firm and unswerving principles.

When the professor got to the last attribute of Paul, the *l* that stood for *loving*, he did not say that Paul was uncompromising *and* loving. He said that Paul was uncompromising, *therefore* loving. He explained that people who compromise their integrity to satisfy other people do not do it because they love them. They may do it because they fear other people or want others to love them.

Paul's love was not like that; his love was more like the love of God. God's love is uncompromising. God does not bend His own character to accommodate us. He has no need to impress us. His love never compromises His holiness or His righteousness. His love is a pure love that cannot be contaminated by our distortions of love.

People use love as an excuse for all kinds of sin. Adultery usually begins with a declaration of love. But the love of God is not adulterous and is not bound by the selfish forms of love that we mix with our human love. God's love rises above pettiness.

If we cannot reverse the order of the words "God is love," what is the meaning of the phrase? In the declaration "God is love" we find a Hebrew mode of expression, a literary device that shows supreme emphasis. To say that God is love is to say that love is so much a part of the character of God and He is so loving that to express the depths of His love we must say He *is* love.

Love, *agape* love, is such an integral part of God's character that John sees an intimate relationship between knowing God and expressing this kind of love ourselves. We are commanded to love one another because love is of God. John says, "He who does not love does not know God" (1 John 4:8). To know God is to learn about *agape*, a special kind of love that goes beyond mere friendship. It is a spiritual love, the kind of love Paul describes in the great love chapter of the Bible, 1 Corinthians 13.

To know God is to know Him in His love. This is not an abstract concept of philosophers. God is no naked thought. He is the Lover of my soul and the One who to know is to love and to learn how to love.

A Giving Love

When the Bible speaks of God's love it invariably reaches the subject of God's sacrificial kindness. The love of God is the love of a God who gives. The most famous verse in the Bible underscores this fact: "God so loved the world that He gave" (John 3:16). This giving of His only begotten Son on our behalf is the dearest expression of the love of God we can find.

The Apostle John wrote, "In this the love of God was manifested toward us, that God has sent His only begotten Son into the world, that we might live through Him" (1 John 4:9). Here John spoke of "manifesting" something. To manifest something is to make it plain, to show it clearly. God doesn't merely talk about being loving; He puts His love to the test by showing it in a way that is undeniable. He shows His love by giving.

What God gives and to whom He gives it further manifests His love. God is a gift-giving God, but His supreme love is shown by His supreme gift—His only begotten Son. Elsewhere Scripture says that there is no greater love than a love that willingly lays down its life for a friend. To sacrifice your life for your friends is the "greatest" display of love we can show. Or is it? Jesus took it one step further by giving His life for His enemies.

Although Jesus did lay down His life for His friends, He died for them while they were still sinners in the midst of deserting and denying Him. This act of self-sacrifice was not done alone. Jesus acted in concert with His Father. In fact, it was His Father's idea. The Father conceived the cup, filled the cup, and gave the cup to the Son to drink. The Son shuddered before the cup and sought to have it removed. The Father said no, He would not compromise. The Son then willingly took the cup and drank it to its bitter dregs. Together they made the gift of Jesus' precious life.

John understood the order, "In this is love, not that we loved God, but that He loved us and sent His Son to be the propitiation for our sins" (1 John 4:10). The essence of the gospel is found in the words, "While we were yet sinners." The love of God reaches out to us while we are alienated from Him. We have no love for Him, and our hearts are stony and cold. We love ourselves and our things. There is no affection in our hearts for God.

The supreme irony is that although God is altogether lovely, as fallen creatures we do not love Him. He is worthy and deserves our love. We owe Him our love, yet we do not love Him. On the other side, we are altogether unlovely by His standards. There is nothing in us to commend us to God, and He certainly does not owe us His love. But the staggering fact remains, *He loves us*. He loves us to the extent that He gave His only begotten Son for us.

We remember the test of Abraham. After God blessed Abraham and Sarah with the child of promise, God called Abraham saying, "'Take now your son, your only son Isaac, whom you love, and go to the land of Moriah, and offer him there as a burnt offering on one of the mountains of which I shall tell you'" (Gen. 22:2).

I wonder what would have happened if God had been more vague and said to Abraham, "Take your son and offer him up to me." With that less specific command I am sure Abraham would have headed straight for Ishmael and taken him on the trip to Mount Moriah. But God was clear; His command was specific: Take your son. Your only son, the son you love, Isaac.

We know how the dreadful test turned out. After Abraham went to the mountain, after he tied Isaac to the altar and raised his knife to slay him, the angel came and told him to release the boy. Abraham's willingness to sacrifice the one he loved the most was enough. God did not make him go through with it.

Centuries later God sent His Son, His only Son, the One whom He loved, Jesus. But this time no angel came, and no one yelled stop!

A Forgiving Love

The Bible reveals that God's love is a forgiving love. The love we experience from humans is always clouded by fear. We never know for sure that the love we are receiving will last. We watch couples break up, friendships shatter, and families tear apart. No love that we experience on earth is totally and absolutely secure. We seek to tighten our commitments by formalizing them with sacred and solemn covenants. But even these covenants sealed with holy vows fall short of giving us the absolute security we seek. Vows can be broken. Love can be broken. We can be broken.

When human love is broken, it is difficult to repair. A broken marriage is hard to reglue. When our love is violated the pain may be so great that we dare not risk another broken heart.

The love that has the power to forgive is as priceless as it is rare. This kind of love keeps on loving even when that love is not returned. This is the love God showed to His people Israel in the Old Testament. It is the kind of love a faithful spouse may give to an unfaithful spouse. The Bible story of the marriage of Hosea to a harlot is an object lesson of God's love for us:

> When the LORD began to speak by Hosea, the LORD said to
>   Hosea:
> "Go, take yourself a wife of harlotry
> And children of harlotry,
> For the land has committed great harlotry
> By departing from the LORD." *(Hosea 1:2)*

When Hosea obeyed the Lord we do not know if Gomer reformed her way of life or if she continued in her harlotry. We do know that Israel continued to disobey God and turned aside to other gods. Yet God's love for Israel remained constant.

At the end of the book of Hosea, God gave this promise to His people:

"I will heal their backsliding,
I will love them freely,
For My anger has turned away from him.
I will be like the dew to Israel;
He shall grow like the lily,
And lengthen his roots like Lebanon.
His branches shall spread;
His beauty shall be like an olive tree,
And his fragrance like Lebanon."   *(Hosea 14:4–5)*

The God of Israel is a God of forgiving love.

Love without Malice

In his great love chapter in 1 Corinthians 13, the Apostle Paul wrote, love "thinks no evil" (v. 5). Jonathan Edwards correctly saw in this statement a kind of love that is the opposite of a censorious spirit. God's love is that of a judge, but it is not a judgmental love.

A judgmental spirit makes snap judgments and delights in finding fault. It basks in criticism. It revels in negative attacks of people. It enjoys thinking the worst of people. The judgmental spirit wears no smile.

The television preacher, Jim Bakker, once announced he would preach about thieves running loose in the church. I assumed that he was about to launch a tirade about finances. I expected him to decry those who withhold their tithes, who systematically and consistently rob God by resisting the offering plate.

As I waited for the dramatic fund appeal, the appeal never came. Jim Bakker was not talking about money nor tithing. He was talking about thieves who were stealing happiness. Bakker called this gang of thieves the "sourpusses" of the church.

We all know sourpusses. They do their stealing under a cloak of piety. There is always a spiritual reason, a theological justification for their judgment. Their fierce scowls and bony, pointing fingers are masked in platitudes of false love. Their criticisms are always "given in love." But they wield knives that are dripping with the blood of their victims. They assault the souls of Christ's lambs. In a word, the judgments they pass are judgments of *malice*.

There is judgment in God. There is wrath in God. God punishes sin. But there is no malice in God, and His judgment is always circumscribed by His love.

I am writing these words in a restaurant. A juke box is playing, and I am trying to concentrate on the yellow legal pad in front of me. A waiter just appeared with my favorite libation, a glass of iced tea—without lemon. As he placed the tea on the table, he noticed my writing and asked, "Are you a critic?"

"No," I replied. My answer was a half-truth. At the moment I am criticizing the critics. I am criticizing a special type of critic—those who labor without love. When I think of such critics, I struggle with my own spirit. It is hard to respond to malice without feeling some of it yourself. Smiling at a sourpuss is hard.

Recently, I was in Philadelphia for a conference for clergymen. The first evening I was talking with some ministers in the hotel lobby when our discussion was interrupted by a parade. We discovered that our hotel was the site of the annual Gay Prom, and about one hundred couples marched by us into the ballroom. The men had tuxedoes; their dates wore elaborate formal gowns. Many of the "ladies" in gowns sported thick mustaches. It was a disturbing sight.

One of the wives present said disgustedly, "Sick, sick, sick." The next day she told me, "Last night I felt only contempt for those gays who were flaunting their distortion. But when I went to my room my feelings changed. I felt only compassion."

Her attitude may be labeled "patronizing" by the homosexual community. But I think she experienced a victory of grace over malice.

One does not need to approve what one loves. I am sure God did not approve of the gay parade. He does not approve of any form of sin. Yet somehow God has an ability to love the unlovely and to care for those whose lives are wicked. If I had to wait for God to approve of everything I did before He could love me, I would still be a lost person. It is while we are still sinners that He loves us. That's a truth none of us dares forget.

The warnings of Jesus against a judgmental spirit are terrifying. He warned us that we are vulnerable to a divine justice that will judge us in the same manner we judge others (see Matt. 7:1–5). I hope Jesus was using hyperbole at that point. If He was speaking in absolute terms, I am in deep trouble. I have been guilty of malice toward others; what if He treats me the same way? I will find no place in His kingdom. My hope is that He will deal with me according to His loving-kindness.

Every pagan in America knows that the Bible says, "Judge not lest ye be judged" (see Matt. 7:1). The world knows Jesus said that. I knew it when I was thirteen, long before I became a Christian, long before I ever read the Bible. At the time I was working in a shoeshine shop as a shineboy. The proprietor was Roman Catholic, and every evening he turned the shop radio to "The Catholic Hour." I learned to shine shoes to the rhythm of the rosary. One evening I heard a priest, whose name was Father Boat, give a scathing attack against Protestants. One phrase kept going through my mind, "Father Boat, remove the mote."

Somewhere I had heard the story Jesus told about the man who was critical of the speck in his brother's eye while having a mote or a log in his own eye. I understood that Jesus was talking about something like black pots and black kettles.

Jonathan Edwards once remarked:

> If men were humbly sensible of their own failings, they would not be very forward or pleased in judging others, for the censure passed upon others would but rest on themselves. There are the same kinds of corruption in one man's heart as in another's; and if those persons that are most busy in censuring others would but look within, and seriously examine their own hearts and lives, they might generally see the same dispositions and behaviour in themselves, at one time or another, which they see and judge in others, or at least something as much deserving of censure. And a disposition to judge and condemn shows a conceited and arrogant disposition.*

*Jonathan Edwards, *Charity and Its Fruits* (Carlisle, PA: The Banner of Truth Trust), 215–216.

Edward's last sentence is worth a closer look. "And a disposition to judge and condemn shows a conceited and arrogant disposition." Notice that Edwards speaks of judging *and* condemning. When Jesus said, "Judge not," what did He mean? Obviously, He did not mean that Christians are not to be aware of evil. Christians must be able to discern the difference between good and evil. How else could we approve what is good?

Jesus was speaking here of a judgmental spirit, a spirit of malice whereby people are summarily condemned by an uncompassionate and arrogant heart. He was speaking of judgment without love.

Judgments of Charity

Preachers, teachers, and authors have a tendency to repeat themselves. We like to beat the same drum over and over again. I take comfort in the knowledge that Jesus, the Master Teacher, also preached the same message on more than one occasion.

In my book *In Search of Dignity,* (Ventura, CA: Regal, 1983), I labored the point of the judgment of charity. Some of that material bears repetition here. If Christians are going to manifest the love of God to a dying world, we need to understand and to practice the judgment of charity.

A judgment of charity is simply a judgment of love. It is the Golden Rule with skin on it. The judgment of charity involves the difference between a worst-case analysis and a best-case analysis. A worst-case analysis means that when we are injured or offended by someone, we impute the worst of all possible motives to the person who hurt us. We view his actions as being as wicked as possible. We assume that our antagonist has stayed up late at night plotting his plan to hurt us. The truth is, however, that most of the wounds inflicted upon us have been caused by people who had no idea how much they were hurting us. We tend to feel far more malice than actually exists. To be sure there are people who do conspire to hurt us. But they are a minority.

As a person known by the public, I receive my share of hate mail. Every author, every speaker, every minister gets vicious letters, and there are different ways to deal with them. Some

Bless the Lord, O my soul;
And all that is within me, bless His holy name!
Bless the Lord, O my soul,
And forget not all His benefits:
Who forgives all your iniquities,
Who heals all your diseases,
Who redeems your life from destruction,
Who crowns you with lovingkindness and tender mercies,
Who satisfies your mouth with good things,
So that your youth is renewed like the eagle's.

. . . .

The Lord is merciful and gracious,
Slow to anger, and abounding in mercy.
He will not always strive with us,
Nor will He keep His anger forever.
He has not dealt with us according to our sins,
Nor punished us according to our iniquities.
For as the heavens are high above the earth,
So great is His mercy toward those who fear Him;
As far as the east is from the west,
So far has He removed our transgressions from us.

Psalm 103:1–5, 8–12

people take the time to answer every charge, every criticism with a painstaking reply. I don't. I've had so many hate letters that now I don't reply to them. But when I was still answering them, I developed a successful technique. When I would receive a blistering letter, I would circle the harsh words with a red pen and return the letter to the sender with this question: "Did you really mean to be this severe? If so, return your letter once again to me and I will reply."

Only once did such a letter-writer respond—with a sheepish letter of apology. We all say things when we are angry that later only embarrass us. Sometimes the most effective letters are the ones never sent.

The judgment of charity gives the benefit of doubt. Sadly, this judgment is all too often reserved for ourselves. That is, we tend to judge ourselves in the best possible light; we want people to be patient and understanding toward our sins. We often think, *If they knew all the facts, they would not judge me so harshly.*

That street runs in both directions. If we want people to judge us with charity, if we want people to give us the benefit of a best-case analysis, then we must be willing to do the same for them. That is what the Golden Rule is all about.

Heavenly Love

There is no hate in heaven. When every other spiritual gift has passed away, there is one that abides. Love endures forever. In my Father's house there is no lack of love. Again, I turn to Edwards to enlarge my own understanding.

> And this renders heaven a world of love; for God is the fountain of love, as the sun is the fountain of light. And therefore the glorious presence of God in heaven, fills heaven with love, as the sun, placed in the midst of the visible heavens in a clear day, fills the world with light. The apostle tells us that "God is love"; and therefore, seeing he is an infinite being, it follows that he is an infinite fountain of love. Seeing he is an all-sufficient being, it follows that he is a full and overflowing, and inexhaustible fountain of love. And in that he is an unchangeable and eternal being, he is an unchangeable and eternal fountain of love.*

The love of God is an expression of all that He is. His love transcends the petty and the fickle. His is a love that will not

---

*Edwards, 326–327.

let us go, a love that fulfills its commitment. God does not divorce His bride. His love is as He is, from everlasting to everlasting, absolutely secure.

The Name above All Names

I was a Roman-numeraled baby. My parents had Robert Charles Sproul, III, written on my birth certificate. It was a cruel thing to do to a boy. All that *III* did was elicit snickers on every formal occasion when it was mentioned. At least, I thought I heard snickers. I heard them at my confirmation, at my graduation, and at my ordination. Someone will surely snicker when they read my name in the obituary column.

I don't know why my parents ever tacked that Roman numeral on my name. For that matter I'm not sure why I received the other parts of my name. In my entire life only one person has ever called me Robert, and no one has called me Charles, although one person did refer to me constantly as Charley.

From the day I was born, to my parents I was R. C. Soon, however, other nicknames came into play. The kids called me Sonny, and for some unknown reason my father called me Luke. (This was an abbreviated version of the full sorbriquet, Luke McGluke.)

Other names appeared. An aunt called me Robby, and in high school I started to sign my name Bob. In baseball I was Rabbit (No, not Scooter). In hockey I was Whip. Later, my wife called me Robin.

Pretty soon I answered to almost anything. Let's review the list: Robert, Robby, Bob, R. C., Sonny, Luke, Rabbit, Whip, Robin, Charley. Those are too many names for one person. Yet I am sure your story is much the same as mine. We all have several names, and each name has a special meaning. Though we answer to more than one name, our names and nicknames are still limited.

God has many, too. The Bible reveals several of them to us, and each of them captures some special dimension of God's character.

At the same time God also has a limited number of names. There are some names that He will not respond to. God has a distinctive personality. He regards it as a grave insult to be confused with other gods. The Hebrew *Shema* stresses the singular character of God: "Hear, O Israel: The LORD our God, the LORD is one!" (Deut. 6:4).

God is one. He is only one. He has different names, but He Himself is one. He must not be confused with false gods. The Ten Commandments begin with a sober rule: "You shall have no other gods before Me" (Exod. 20:3). At the very beginning God guards us against slipping into the sin of idolatry.

What did God mean by "before Me"? God may seem to have said He must rank #1 on our list of gods. Is it all right with God to have many gods on our list as long as He ranks in first place? On the contrary, the "before Me" does not refer to an order or rank. The "before" refers to a location. God is saying here, "You shall have no other gods in My presence."

It is fashionable to say that God reveals Himself by many names, meaning that we all worship the same god. We may call Him Jehovah, but other people call Him Brahma or Buddha or Confucius. This idea is very popular in a world that is tired of religious debates and wars. The simple solution to the conflict between religions is to merge them into one, to declare that all religions are basically the same. "We all worship the same God, we merely call Him by a different name."

Such a view of God goes far to achieve human peace; however, it does so at the high risk of offending God. God is jealous about His name. He is even more jealous about His identity. God does not like to be confused with idols. He has many names, to be sure, but there are some names to which He will not respond. His name is not Baal. He does not answer to Dagon. His attention is not given to the name Buddha.

Do you remember Elijah and the prophets of Baal in 1 Kings 18? They faced a moment of national crisis. The people were getting confused with religion; too many gods were competing for their allegiance. Elijah stepped forward with a crucial challenge: "How long will you falter between two opinions? If the LORD is God, follow Him; but if Baal, then follow him" (v. 21).

The challenge was followed by a contest. The God of Israel, Yahweh, would face the god of the Canaanites, Baal. The stakes for the contest were established. The crowd gathered. The priests of Baal called on their god first:

> So they took the bull which was given them, and they prepared it, and called on the name of Baal from morning even till noon, saying, "O Baal, hear us!" But there was no voice; no one answered. And they leaped about the altar which they had made. *(v. 26)*

No one answered. If someone calls me R. C., I will answer. If they call me Bob, I'll answer to that, too. But if someone calls me Walter, I'll assume they are talking to somebody else. I don't answer to that name. In the same way, God doesn't answer to the name Baal. Baal had devoted followers. He had priests. He had temples named after him. He had statues fashioned to look like him. He had a catch-name. The only thing that he lacked was existence. Baal didn't exist except in the people's imagination.

Elijah responded to the priests of Baal by mocking them: "And so it was, at noon, that Elijah mocked them and said, 'Cry aloud, for he is a god; either he is meditating, or he is busy, or he is on a journey, or perhaps he is sleeping and must be awakened'" (v. 27).

Something was wrong with Baal's ears. Somehow he was unable to hear the pleas of his priests. Elijah suggested several excuses for him. None gave much comfort to the priests. They grew desperate with their pleading. They resorted to screaming and cut themselves with knives and lances. This accomplished nothing. They were calling upon the wrong name. The Lord God of heaven does not respond to the name Baal.

God did respond to Elijah:

> And it came to pass, at the time of the offering of the evening sacrifice, that Elijah the prophet came near and said, "LORD God of Abraham, Isaac, and Israel, let it be known this day that You are God in Israel, and that I am Your servant, and that I have done all these things at Your word." *(v. 36)*

Elijah addressed God by name. God heard his prayer and answered him. Fire fell from heaven, and God vindicated His holy name. The response of the people is noteworthy: "Now when all the people saw it, they fell on their faces; and they said, 'The LORD, He is God! The LORD, He is God!'" (v. 39).

When the fire fell from heaven the first thing the people did was fall on their faces. This is the appropriate response to the true God. The god who can be called by any name drives nobody to his knees. The god with a million names is feared by no one. Only Yahweh, the God of Israel, the Holy One, puts people on their knees.

The second thing the fire from heaven did was to make the people cry out the name of God: "The LORD, He is God." The meaning of this phrase is, "Yahweh, He is God."

God Is Jealous—for His Name

Few of us enjoy having our names mispronounced. When someone calls me "Sprowl . . . rhymes with growl," I feel like someone has scratched his fingernails along a blackboard. My name rhymes with *soul*, and I hate to hear it said any other way.

But if someone mispronounces my name—what's the harm? My ego may sting a bit, but no theological crisis follows. God's name is different. His name is sacred, is protected by weighty sanctions, and is to be honored. The law of God requires that His name not be taken in vain. God's names reveal something of His person. His names are important.

The most common name for God in the ancient Near East was the generic *El*. This simple name was used by the Jews and by other nations as well. It was similar to our word *God*. Although its origin is uncertain, most scholars agree that its root meaning is related to strength. El has been translated "mighty," "prominent," or simply "the first One."

El appears often in the Bible in connection with Hebrew places and names—Bethel, Daniel, Ezekiel, and Israel. Bethel is "the house of God." Daniel means "God is my Judge." Ezekiel means "God strengthens." Israel means "prince with God."

In its plural form the name *El* takes on a mysterious and controversial character. One of the earliest names for God found in the Bible is *Elohim*. Here God's name is plural and literally can be translated "Gods." This is the name of God we meet in creation: "Then God said, 'Let *Us* make man in *Our* image, according to Our likeness'" (Gen. 1:26, italics mine).

How are we to understand this? Does the plural form suggest that in the early stages of Hebrew religion the Jewish people embraced a crude form of polytheism? In its infancy does the Bible imitate a kind of religion found in other parts of the world?

We are familiar with the polytheistic religion of the Greeks and the Romans. These cultures had special deities for special concerns. There was a god of war, a god of love, a god of wisdom, a god of hunting, and so on. To this day we hear their names—Mars, Jupiter, Mercury, Venus, Juno, Diana, and Vesta. A god could be found for every need.

The same plurality of gods could be found in Norse religion, in Egypt, and in India. Were the Jews any different?

Critics of biblical faith argue that the idea of monotheism, of belief in one god, was a late development among the Jews. The idea is that all forms of religion, whether Indian, Greek, or Jewish, undergo a long process of evolution. Just as biological forms of life supposedly evolve from the simple to the complex, so man's religions follow the same pattern. "How could this unsophisticated, obscure group of Jewish believers have developed monotheism centuries before anyone else?" the critics ask.

There is much at stake here. If it can be shown that the Jewish people were polytheistic like other nations, then the conclusion follows that at least the early chapters of the Bible reflect human mythology, not divine revelation. If the Bible is based ultimately on mythology, it has no authority to bind us now. It becomes an interesting source of primitive religion but loses its power to proclaim, "Thus saith the Lord."

The problem with this evolutionary view is that it violates the picture of God we find in early Bible history. The idea is malicious and in radical conflict with the biblical text itself. That the God of Israel is One and that He is the Creator of the whole world is interwoven in the fabric of the Old Testament so thoroughly that only a vandal with a pair of scissors could crudely rip it out.

Yet, why is that plural form of God used in the first chapter of Genesis? The customary conservative Christian response to the critic is to say, "Oh, here we have an early revelation of the Trinity, that's all."

This is a tempting reply, but finding the Trinity neatly revealed here also does violence to the text and language of Scripture. To be sure the concept of Trinity is compatible with the name *Elohim*, and in an indirect way the idea of Trinity is vaguely and obscurely hinted at in the text. However, we go too far if we say that the biblical author's chief purpose in using Elohim was to indicate Trinity.

Hebrew scholars offer the suggestion that in the plural use of Elohim is a plural of intensity. There is an inner richness to the character and being of God. God is one—He is not made up of seventeen separate parts—yet in His oneness there is a multiplicity of nuances and attributes. God is not one-dimensional. The plural of intensity, therefore, displays the fullness of life and power within God.

Notably the plural form of Elohim is used in the Bible with singular verbs and singular adjectives. Elohim is a name for a single God. He has one identity, one being, one character. But He is a God who has within Himself a fullness that is rich in meaning.

In God we find the One who has within Himself the foundation of all unity and diversity. *Unity* and *diversity* are abstract terms, and we seldom devote much serious thought to them. These are concepts for philosophers to wrestle with.

But resolving the tensions streaming from unity and diversity is a crucial challenge of our day. The problem of unity and diversity has political, social, educational, and ethical ramifications. It is the issue behind the civil rights struggle, the feminist movement, the abortion question, and every other issue that divides us.

There is an ugly-sounding word that captures one of the current problems of unity and diversity. The word comes into our language from the Dutch, by way of South Africa. It is *apartheid*. The word's simple meaning is "apartness." It involves the separation of people who are different from one another.

I have never been to South Africa and *apartheid* is a foreign word to me. But I encountered its meaning in high school.

It was October of 1955. At 6:15 P.M. the sky was already dark, and the evening air had a biting chill. I walked out of the cavernous underbelly of Clairton Stadium, my hair still wet from the shower, and headed toward downtown Clairton with my best friend, "Philco" Batten, a fleet-footed halfback who was the star of our football team.

As we passed Walker's Drugstore I said, "Hey Phil, let's go in and get a Coke. My mouth tastes like leather."

A strange look appeared on Philco's face. I saw a slight glint of fear that I hadn't seen there before. He shrugged and feigned a nonchalant reply, "No, man. Let's skip it."

In my naiveté I missed Philco's veiled warning and continued to press. I finally persuaded my reluctant friend to enter the store. We approached the soda fountain and sat on the plastic red-capped swivel stools. I spoke to the soda jerk, "Two Cokes, please."

Moments later the soda jerk returned with one Coke. He placed it in front of me. "Where's Phil's Coke?" I said.

The soda jerk nodded over his shoulder to the manager who was standing with arms folded and a mean leer on his face. He stepped forward and said, "We don't serve colored."

Then directing his comments to Philco he said, "You know better than to come in here, boy."

Again he looked at me and said, "Now finish your Coke and get out of here!"

That was my first experience with apartheid. It was not in South Africa. It was not in Mississippi. It was in Pennsylvania, in the industrial northeast.

I left the drug store enraged, recoiling at this blatant injustice. I had witnessed an assault against a human being's dignity based on racial discrimination. The store owner had no room in his life-system for diversity. Philco was different. He didn't belong.

Obviously, the store owner did not understand the character of God. He did not know Elohim, the Creator who made both blacks and whites in His own image.

The God of the Universe

The Bible says that in the beginning God made the heavens and the earth. The message is clear: God made everything that is. He did not make part of the universe for white people and the other part for black people. Nor is He the Creator only of one section of town while allowing some subdeity to be Creator and Lord of the ghetto. Elohim is the Lord God over all. The whole world is His and everything in it. It is because God made everything that we call His creation a *universe*.

What is a universe? The word itself has a strange, mixed pedigree. The two words *unity* and *diversity* are jammed together to make one word. A universe, then, is a place where all sorts of diverse things are fitted together to make a unified whole.

In the universe we find oceans, rivers, streams, and puddles. We find mountains, hills, slopes, and valleys. There are fish, plants, kangaroos, and spiders. We find rocks, baseballs, garters, and chocolate bars. There are men, women, babies, and gorillas. There are white, blue, red, and pink things. There are little, medium, and giant, economy-sized things. In a word, we find *diversity*.

But how does all this fit together? Or does it? Does this wide variety of people, places, and things make sense or is it all a jumbled mass of chaos? Is there an ultimate order or ultimate nonsense?

I remember a rebuke I once received from a seminary professor. One class assignment was to put together a Sunday school lesson for children. I tried to make a game of the morning lesson and created a simple crossword puzzle for the children to complete. My professor objected: "The subtle message you are sending to the children is that life is a puzzle and the church has the answer to the puzzle."

I was surprised. *Is it wrong,* I wondered, *ever to suggest that the Christian faith might dare answer any ultimate questions?* The professor was committed to a philosophy of always learning but never coming to a knowledge of truth.

I replied, "But, sir, life is a puzzle. And if we don't have any answers to that puzzle, what in the world are we doing here?"

This conversation reminded me of Erasmus's chiding Martin Luther for making assertions. Luther replied in fury, "Take away assertions and you take away Christianity. The Holy Spirit is not a skeptic."

The professor was echoing the spirit of our age. We live in a time of the eclipse of God. God is so far removed from our thinking that we no longer see the unity of diversity. We hear the cry of the teachers who declare that there are no absolutes and the voices of the cynics who see all life as meaningless.

This trend in our culture is no more evident than in the modern university. (There is that mongrel word again.) A university is supposedly a place where we learn about our universe. Many subjects are studied. Our schools offer courses in geology, biology, and anthropology. We study law, medicine, music, and engineering.

Why, then, don't we call our colleges "multiversities"? Universities were originally called universities because the assumption of scholars and scientists was that true knowledge makes sense. It is coherent. It is consistent. It all fits together. In a word, all true knowledge is unified.

Those were the original assumptions of higher education. But those assumptions are now under siege, and our modern university system is in a state of severe crisis. The modern student goes from class to class learning individual pieces of the puzzle, but the pieces never seem to fit together into a unified whole. Going from the astronomy class to the fraternity or sorority hour, the student switches from a discussion of exploding novae to a discussion of astrological signs. The result is intellectual chaos.

The modern student learns one view of man in biology class and a contradictory view of man in psychology class. The conflict is resolved with a bottle of liquor or a noseful of cocaine. Students are confused, angry, and depressed. The teachers have despaired of coming to an understanding of truth. Our universities are held captive by skepticism, and the students are the hostages.

Knowledge of particulars without any overarching basis of unity is a kind of intellectual terrorism. The mind is abducted and forced into a torture chamber. The student seeking answers is battered with diversity with no hope of unity. Education has become an ordeal for someone searching for ultimate truth.

In the classical university, theology was regarded as the queen of the sciences and received royal respect because she alone held the keys to ultimate unity. But the queen has been rudely dethroned. She has been systematically raped and banished into exile. She is not dead, but she has been stripped of her authority. She may speak only to her loyal subjects who are likewise confined to her tiny island kingdom. She may no longer speak in the schools. She is not considered in the vote. She has no authority in court.

Modern humanity faces a multiverse. Life no longer makes sense, and many do not even try to find ultimate answers. They have stopped thinking and are content just to live, to strut an hour upon the stage and then not be heard from again. Life keeps them busy and is lived on the rim of intoxication. Finally, there is the surrender to the idiot's tale, the tale of sound and fury, signifying nothing.

Mankind still feels, still cares, still marches in protest. But why? Are we fulfilling the prophecy of doom uttered by Socrates: "The unexamined life is not worth living"?

The examined life must look beyond particulars. We must rise above the diversity to discover ultimate unity. To achieve that we must recall our queen. We must liberate her from her captivity. Nothing less will do. Only a theological view of life will give us a unified view of life. Only God can resolve disharmony. Only in Him can diversity find unity. Without the infinite we perish with the finite. Without the Absolute, we drown in the relative. Without the Author of order, we suffocate in chaos.

Elohim, the God who has the basis of unity and diversity within Himself, makes sense of the world in which we live. A coherent understanding of life requires a coherent understanding of God. To know Him is to learn who we are and what the world is all about. Knowing Him must become a holy passion within us. It must fill our frame. It must engage our mind. Religion is inescapable, because mankind is incurably religious. Take away the true God and we are left with an intolerable vacuum, a vacuum that we and nature abhor. It must be filled. If God is banished, idols will rush in to fill the void.

The Apostle Paul declared that the most fundamental of all sins was idolatry. We are, as Calvin described it, human idol-factories. We turn out idols in mass production. We build assembly lines for them. Our tendency toward idolatry is so strong that we must be on constant red alert to it. We are vulnerable to its seduction, and conversion to Christian faith is no guarantee against it.

Idolatry is more than crude totem poles, bronze images, and plastic statues. If these were the scope of idolatry, we would not need to be so concerned. But there are more subtle forms of idolatry, which simply is the worship of things that are less than God. It is obvious to us that men and trees are less than God, as are golden calves. But what if our concept of God is less than the biblical concept of God? God with all of His attributes is the biblical God. We must be sure that our concept of God includes all that the Bible teaches about Him.

I shudder when I hear professing Christians reject the sovereignty of God or the justice of God. "But my God is a God of love," some say, as if God's character could be exhausted by one attribute. Here the attribute of love is so exalted that it swallows up God's other attributes. The result is a one-dimensional God, a God who is less than God, an idol.

The God we love and worship is a God of depth and fullness. He is one and many. He has unity and diversity. He is one being with several attributes. In this life we only begin to understand the depth and the riches of His being. We only skate on the surface of understanding Him.

The more we search the Scriptures the deeper we should move in our understanding of God. The more we know Him, the more we understand how worthy He is of our worship. We adore Him because He is adorable. We honor Him because He is honorable. We love Him because He is altogether lovely.

His majesty fills the world. His wisdom governs our lives. His mercy forgives our sins. His immutability keeps and preserves us. His omnipotence enlightens our darkness. In

Him we live and move and have our being. He is our God and we are His people.

To God Be the Glory

O GOD, You are my God;
Early will I seek You;
My soul thirsts for You;
My flesh longs for You
In a dry and thirsty land
Where there is no water.
So I have looked for You in the sanctuary,
To see Your power and Your glory.
Because Your lovingkindness is better than life,
My lips shall praise You.
Thus I will bless You while I live;
I will lift up my hands in Your name.
My soul shall be satisfied as with marrow and fatness,
And my mouth shall praise You with joyful lips.
When I remember You on my bed,
I meditate on You in the night watches.
Because You have been my help,
Therefore in the shadow of Your wings I will rejoice.
My soul follows close behind You;
Your right hand upholds me.
But those who seek my life, to destroy it,
Shall go into the lower parts of the earth.
They shall fall by the sword;
They shall be a portion for jackals.
But the king shall rejoice in God;
Everyone who swears by Him shall glory;
But the mouth of those who speak lies shall be stopped.

Psalm 63

ABOUT R. C. SPROUL

Dr. R. C. Sproul is a nationally recognized theologian who is known for his ability to communicate deep truths in a fresh and easy to understand style. The president of Ligonier Ministries in Orlando, Florida, which provides biblical instruction for laypersons, Dr. Sproul is currently professor of systematic theology and apologetics at Reformed Theological Seminary. He lectures nationwide and has an extensive audio and video tape teaching ministry. Dr. Sproul is the author of eighteen books, including The Holiness of God, Knowing Scripture, *and* Reason to Believe.

For more information about Dr. Sproul or his ministry
write:

P.O. Box 7500
Orlando, Florida 32854